Stanley Kubrick
and the Art of Adaptation

Stanley Kubrick and the Art of Adaptation

Three Novels, Three Films

Greg Jenkins

McFarland & Company, Inc., Publishers
Jefferson, North Carolina, and London

The present work is a reprint of the library bound edition of Stanley Kubrick and the Art of Adaptation: Three Novels, Three Films, *first published in 1997 by McFarland.*

LIBRARY OF CONGRESS CATALOGUING-IN-PUBLICATION DATA

Jenkins, Greg, 1952–
    Stanley Kubrick and the art of adaptation : three novels, three films / Greg Jenkins.
        p.   cm.
    Includes bibliographical references and index.

    ISBN-13: 978-0-7864-3097-0
    (softcover : 50# alkaline paper) ∞

    1. Film adaptations.   2. Kubrick, Stanley—Criticism and interpretation.   3. Nabokov, Vladimir Vladimirovich, 1899–1977—Film and video adaptations.   4. King, Stephen, 1947–   —Film and video adaptations.   5. Hasford, Gustav—Film and video adaptations.   I. Title.
PN1997.85.J46   2007
791.43'0233'092—dc21   96-37164

British Library cataloguing data are available

©1997 Greg Jenkins. All rights reserved

No part of this book may be reproduced or transmitted in any form or by any means, electronic or mechanical, including photocopying or recording, or by any information storage and retrieval system, without permission in writing from the publisher.

On the cover: Stanley Kubrick on the set of *The Shining*, 1980 (Warner Brothers/Photofest); Sue Lyon in *Lolita*, 1962 (MGM/Photofest); Jack Nicholson in *The Shining;* and R. Lee Ermey in *Full Metal Jacket*, 1987 (Warner Brothers/Photofest)

Manufactured in the United States of America

McFarland & Company, Inc., Publishers
    Box 611, Jefferson, North Carolina 28640
        www.mcfarlandpub.com

To Michelle

Adaptation is a peculiar form of discourse but not
an unthinkable one. —*Dudley Andrew*

Contents

Chapter 1. *Introduction* — 1
  The Problem of Adaptation — 3
  Statements on Adaptation — 8
    Journalistic Positions — 9
    Scholarly Positions — 13
    Practical Positions — 20
    Kubrick's Position — 23
  Approach and Method — 25

Chapter 2. *Lolita* — 31
  Prelude — 34
  Lolita Discovered — 37
  Lolita Acquired — 48
  Beardsley — 54
  Flight from Beardsley — 59
  Finale — 64

Chapter 3. *The Shining* — 69
  Exposition — 73
  Closing Day — 78
  The Crisis Foreshadowed — 81
  The Crisis Realized — 87
  Climax and Resolution — 99

Chapter 4. *Full Metal Jacket* — 107
  Parris Island — 110
    Exposition — 110

Pyle as Albatross	115
Pyle, Born Again	121
Vietnam	127
Exposition	127
Hue, Cowboy, and the Lusthog Squad	132
The Sniper	140
Chapter 5. *Conclusions*	149
Bibliography	163
Index	171

Chapter 1
Introduction

"Adapting a best-seller for the movies is like carving flesh down to the bone," Richard Corliss has written. "You keep the skeleton, then apply rouge and silicone until the creature looks human" ("Wrong Arm" 58). The assertion, which one presumes is not strictly tied to a novel's sales, has much to recommend it: it is terse, witty, and memorably grotesque. It even contains a substantial measure of truth. But, as I will establish herein, it is a simplistic description of a fairly intricate process; worse, in some specific situations, it is plainly inaccurate.

My object in this book is to explore the long-standing problem of film adaptation. More exactly, I mean to illustrate how selected narratives become altered as they pass from novel to film form and to assay the effects of these alterations. I will dwell mainly on changes in the characters and in narrative structure, since this direction is indicated by the relevant literature, but I will also attend to matters of style, scope, pace, mood, and meaning. My approach, as I explain below, is rhetorical.

I have chosen to focus on three films directed by Stanley Kubrick—*Lolita*, *The Shining*, and *Full Metal Jacket*—and on the novels that inspired them. My reasons for gravitating to Kubrick are straightforward. He is, first, an eminently successful director-screenwriter, the subject of several books and numberless reviews and articles. Norman Kagan submits that Kubrick's oeuvre holds "great critical interest, both in terms of the films' ideas and comments about our culture and society, and in their own aesthetic concerns" (189). Thomas Nelson contends that Kubrick's films "embody such a stylistic and conceptual density that they are capable of stimulating even the most parochial of critical tastes" (1). Gene Phillips notes that Kubrick "has steadily built a reputation as a filmmaker of international importance" (30). With some finality, Alexander Walker has pronounced him a "major artist" (*Kubrick Directs* 44).

Second, Kubrick has evidenced a marked interest in adaptation. As of 1993, he has directed 12 commercial films: *Fear and Desire* (1953), *Killer's Kiss* (1955), *The Killing* (1956), *Paths of Glory* (1957), *Spartacus* (1960), *Lolita* (1961), *Dr. Strangelove, or How I Learned to Stop Worrying and Love the Bomb* (1963), *2001: A Space Odyssey* (1968), *A Clockwork Orange* (1971), *Barry Lyndon* (1975), *The Shining* (1980), and *Full Metal Jacket* (1987). All but the first two are adapted. Of the adaptations, all but *2001*, which is derived from Arthur C. Clarke's short story "The Sentinel," are based on novels (Kolker 400–5). Moreover, Kubrick has been forthcoming in divulging his views of the adaptive art.

Third, as a circle of onlookers univocally attests, Kubrick's ability to control and safeguard his projects is exceptional among directors. As long ago as 1966, Jeremy Bernstein wrote: "Kubrick supervises every aspect of his films, from selecting costumes to choosing the incidental music" (91). Walker discloses that, following the frustrating experience of *Spartacus*, wherein actor Kirk Douglas had ultimate authority, Kubrick has "never relinquished the power of decision-making to anyone" (*Kubrick Directs* 27). Phillips observes that Kubrick has "full artistic control over his films," and that he guides them "from the earliest stages of planning and scripting through the final snap of the editor's shears" (30). Martha Duffy and Richard Schickel confirm that he is unencumbered by "studio advice or interference" (75), and Kagan proclaims him an "auteur critic's dream":

> He writes, shoots, directs, edits, and often handles his own publicity. He has, in fact, sought ever more control as his career [has] progressed; his films are probably as close to personal works of art as any in the commercial cinema [xiii].

Kubrick's estimable power is a point to be remembered since, if he were less commanding, his beliefs concerning adaptation would ring hollow: he would be less able to act on them.

I am aware of just one extended work, a 1982 dissertation by Judy Lee Kinney, that analyzes Kubrick's films expressly as adaptations. (Many shorter studies grapple with the issue, particularly as regards *Lolita*.) While Kinney's treatment is informed and helpful, it is not definitive, and, to a degree, I justify my own effort by enumerating some of the differences between her study and mine:

1. Kinney's literature review, which mentions George Bluestone, André Bazin, and a few others, is quite frugal. I furnish a wider and more detailed conspectus of how adaptation has been understood, recounting statements made by approximately two dozen diverse sources.
2. She discusses six films; I discuss three (including *Full Metal Jacket*, which of course she could not). Whereas her discussion claims greater breadth, mine offers increased depth; my readings are closer.
3. Kinney touches on the novels just lightly. Since, after all, they represent the root of the adaptive process, I bring them more dedicated attention.

Insofar as I view the craggy terrain of adaptation through a limiting window—my perspective is rhetorical and restricted to three films directed by one person—I must concede that none of my findings assumes the form of a universal law. Then again, as the literature makes clear, the topic simply does not lend itself to edicts. Still, in the course of my investigation, a network of trends, which I summarize in my concluding chapter, does emerge. I trust that these trends reveal something fundamental about Stanley Kubrick's adaptive technique, and, by inference, provide a glimmer of insight into the knotty, persistent problem of adaptation at large.

The Problem of Adaptation

Not everyone agrees that adaptation is a "problem"; some have sought (I paraphrase Joyce) to refine the very concept of adaptation out of existence. William Horne, for instance, spreads doubt on the underlying premise of originality, without which adaptation is rendered meaningless. Throughout history, he notes, artists have commonly appropriated available materials and recast them into new incarnations. The tragedians of ancient Greece—Aeschylus, Euripides—fashioned their plays from traditional myths (Horne 21). During the Renaissance and Neoclassical periods, uncounted European writers borrowed "freely and openly" from their predecessors (22). Even Coleridge's strikingly distinctive "Kubla Khan" has its origins in the poet's omnivorous reading (23). One apprehends that, by this reasoning, true originality would mean the creation of a work totally incomprehensible to all but its creator (23–24). Ergo, if nothing is truly original, then nothing is truly adapted.

Dudley Andrew takes a similar tack. Citing the Marxist notion that one's consciousness is not "open to the world," but instead filters the world's substance in accordance with a governing ideology, he concludes that

> every cinematic rendering will exist in relation to some prior whole [that is] lodged unquestioned in the personal or public system of experience. In other words, no filmmaker and no film (at least in the representational mode) responds immediately to reality itself, or to its inner vision. Every representational film *adapts* a prior conception [97].

As such, Andrew discerns a connection between adaptation and interpretation theory, particularly with respect to the so-called hermeneutic circle: "an explication of a text occurs only after a prior understanding of it, yet that prior understanding is justified by the careful explication it allows" (97). In something of a brooding afterthought, he supposes that these speculations "may encourage a hopelessly broad view of adaptation" (97).

I personally find the foregoing arguments not only hopelessly broad but aimlessly sophistical. Adaptation in the narrow sense, the translation of a non-filmic to a filmic text, is a real and identifiable phenomenon. More to the point, it does constitute a problem. Its status as a problem arises from two factors: the sheer prevalence of adapted films and the vexed issue of fidelity. Put differently, adaptations are difficult for the cineast to avoid, and even more difficult to assess in terms of their relationship, normative or otherwise, to the prior text.

From the earliest days of filmmaking, novels have served as a fertile source of screen narratives. Harris Ross reports that the first film adaptation occurred in 1896, with Thomas Edison's excerpting of *The Widow Jones* (1). As film quickly evolved into a popular medium of entertainment, production companies developed an appetite for narrative materials that Horne has called "insatiable" (31). The first adaptation of Conan Doyle's detective stories had appeared by 1900, in the film *Sherlock Holmes Baffled*. By 1910, the fictional sleuth had been featured in some 22 films shown not just in America but in Italy, Hungary, Denmark, France, and Germany (Horne 31). In 1928, Leda Bauer understood that the typical Hollywood "scenario editor" was responsible for

> finding the thrillers in the classics, ... [and] also for a thorough knowledge of the contents of every novel published within the past fifteen years, here or abroad.... This material he is supposed to get in advance of the editors of rival and competitive companies, all of whom are his enemies, spying on his methods, alert to rush in and grab what he has missed [288].

And in 1936, Maxine Block was moved to catalog then recent films made from books, plays, and short stories. Scanning over a period of only three months, she listed 39 films adapted from books alone, with dozens more in the imminent offing (394–95).

Since then, the tendency to adapt has hardly abated. Morris Beja estimated in 1979 that the proportion of films based on novels was roughly 30 percent annually, and "sometimes higher" (78). Harry Geduld, writing in the mid–1960s, put the figure at about 40 percent (qtd. in Ross 1), and Andrew claims that "well over half of all commercial films have come from literary originals" (98). Carrying his appraisal a step further, Beja advised that of the 20 highest-grossing films ever through 1977, 16 were adaptations, and most of those were drawn from novels (78). He judged that a remarkable 80 percent of "best-selling" novels are made into films (78). The most recent edition of *Enser's Filmed Books and Plays* includes 377 densely printed pages listing films, released from 1928 through 1991, that were based on novels or plays (Baskin and Hicken). Indeed, Steven Spielberg's stupendously lucrative *Jurassic Park*, whose worldwide gross in 1993 exceeded $860 million ("Domestic" 24; Groves 30), was shaped from Michael Crichton's novel.

As Maryvonne Butcher observes, the reasons for resorting to adaptation are "manifold and complex" (56), but they may be distilled down to a related pair. First, Hollywood has long been afflicted by a real or perceived dearth of quality stories. Driven by a "sheer lack of confidence in their own creative abilities" (56), film executives have felt compelled to venture outside their immediate realm in search of material. Second, they have seen how a film taken from a novel may enjoy a "bonus of goodwill and potential interest, so that a timid audience will have a head start with the theme" (56); in the words of Gilbert Seldes, filmmakers buy the "prestige and popularity which the book has won" (13). Of course, a book need not be popular—or even published—in order to attract filmdom's attention. A case in point is Scott Smith's first novel, *A Simple Plan*, whose rights were recently acquired by director Mike Nichols "before a single copy [had been] sold" (Max 128). In any event, Hollywood's quest for exogenous source materials, a pursuit that William Fadiman has labeled "frenetic" ("Myth Makers" 30), is by now thoroughly and deeply institutionalized (Macgowan 333–46).

The wrangling over fidelity, an issue so often dissected that Andrew has declared it "tiresome" (100), is likewise entrenched. Philosophic disagreement over how faithful a film should be to its source and what precisely is meant by "faithful" is considerable. Naturally, some changes in a story occur automatically, as a result of dissimilarities between film and other kinds of media. Brian McFarlane cites an unnamed writer's comment: "Film is a multi-sensory communal experience emphasizing immediacy, whereas literature is a mono-sensory experience that is more conducive to reflection" (11). Wolfgang Iser bemoans film's propensity to fill in gaps, as when it presents an unambiguous view of a character's physical appearance:

> While reading *Tom Jones*, [people] may never have a clear conception of what the hero actually looks like, but on seeing the film, some may say, "That's not how I imagined him." The point here is

that the reader of *Tom Jones* is able to visualize the hero ... , and so one's imagination senses the vast number of possibilities; the moment these possibilities are narrowed down to one complete and immutable picture, the imagination is put out of action, and we feel we have somehow been cheated [283].

This ineluctable filling in of gaps aside, some pundits insist that an adapted film should adhere as closely as feasible to its source. Bauer, having noted the various damaging "operations" that may be "inflicted" on a story by Hollywood (294), conjured a sad outcome. Hoping to see a favorite story on screen, the public "sees instead something that only remotely resembles it. [Viewers'] disappointment is none the less keen when the apologists of film point out that translation to the screen requires different symbols, and so on" (294). She brashly predicted that, as a consequence, viewers would begin to eschew theaters "in hordes" (294). Conceding that irreverent adapters "cannot harm the original in the eyes of those who know it" (65), André Bazin nevertheless expressed a preference for the faithful adaptation. In fact, he pinned his hopes for the future of cinema to those who "honestly attempt an integral [film] equivalent" (66), and warranted that a "good adaptation should result in a restoration of the letter and the spirit [of the original]" (67). More currently, Horne refers to "rabid advocates" of strict translation— he names Lester Asheim—who hold that fidelity is "tantamount to a moral duty" (73–74). In the same vein, McFarlane writes:

> Complaints that characters and episodes have been altered or omitted usually suggest that the novel has been "tampered with," as if such a process were vaguely indecent. There is a widespread assumption ... [that] the novel [is] in some sense sacrosanct [1].

Most critics, however, are rather open-minded with respect to the fealty of adaptations. While they expect to notice some affinity between novel and film, the level of fidelity is rarely thrust to the forefront of a critique. Even in 1936, Seldes grasped that "except in the rarest instances ... a good movie cannot be faithful to the original book or play and, conversely, a faithful version cannot be a good movie" (3). A film is primarily visual, he wrote, and gains its effectiveness more from depicted movement than from words or theme (4). He therefore argued that films are at bottom a "separate form, and must be allowed to develop independently, borrowing what they can use, rejecting everything else" (4). Fadiman's concurrence with these sentiments is forceful:

> It is patent that ... [an adapted film] is not deemed to be a mirrored version, a replica, a facsimile, a copy or a resemblance of the original material.... It has become something new.... It is indisputable that the ... motion picture could not exist without the inspiration provided by the play or the novel; but once this [fact] is assumed and accepted, the ensuing film should be criticized strictly within its own frame of reference ["But Compared" 22].

More recently, offering practical advice on screenwriting, Dwight Swain and Joye Swain counsel that following the book meticulously is just one of what they see as three possibilities; the adapter, alternatively, may work from key scenes or may construct an "original" screenplay for which the novel is merely a guide (195–98).

Adaptation, then, is a presence that is woven into the very fabric of film culture. To engage with cinema is to ponder adaptation. Yet it represents such a dark and enigmatic thread that it has elicited disparate and sometimes diametric opinions. Even among those who champion faithful adaptations, there is no clear formula concerning how generally to implement the procedure, or afterwards how to evaluate the procedure's success or failure. Since every adaptive situation is unique—as is every adapter—no such formula is likely to be devised. In sum, adaptation looms as an issue that may and ought to be addressed, probed, weighed, and considered. But, thoroughgoing problem that it is, it can never be fully resolved.

Statements on Adaptation

My purpose in synopsizing a variety of statements regarding adaptation is to give an idea of the history, size, and slippery nature of the problem. This compendium is by no means intended to be exhaustive, if exhaustiveness were even possible. It ranges farther, however, than any single review of the literature I have seen to date. I have selected the comments in accord with my perception of their trenchancy and usefulness—not because they espouse one viewpoint or another. (Kubrick's, obviously, are included for their direct relevance to this project.) Each set of remarks has its merits and shortcomings, but each, I believe, makes an appreciable contribution to the discussion of adaptation.

For the sake of manageability, I have separated the statements into three broad categories—journalistic, scholarly, and practical—and into one narrow category—those promulgated by Stanley Kubrick himself. By "journalistic" I mean statements that have appeared in a popular context, or that have been written in an informal style. "Scholarly" refers to statements made in an academic context: journals, or books exhibiting rigorous research and a formal style. "Practical" denotes statements of a how-to temper, or those offered by practitioners—screenwriters and other Hollywood professionals. The items are arranged chronologically within each category except Kubrick's, moving from earliest to most current.

If Roland Barthes is anywise accurate in framing every text as an interweaving of voices (21), the insight is doubly true for the bumptious literature of adaptation. Here is what some of the voices are saying.

Journalistic Positions

Betraying a cynicism that seems years ahead of her time, Leda Bauer, just prior to the Great Depression, sketched a Hollywood at once desperate for stories and yet inept at handling those it acquired. Beleaguered scenario editors were obliged to canvass "all the material in existence" that might be transferred to the screen (288). Mindful of the ferocious competition among studios, these editors routinely skimmed through novels before their publication, either as proofs or even as raw manuscripts. Once obtained, a story would run a gauntlet of venal, self-interested "advisors": a director, a treatment writer, a writer of originals, all of whom were eager to intrude their own ideas—for money, of course (293). The story, which to Bauer's jaundiced eye was typically "fifth-rate" to begin with, was now completely rewritten, although seldom for the better (294). When it no longer bore any resemblance to the original, it was pronounced "perfect," and given a spicy new title (294). The original story was then resold to another interest, only to be put through the same dreary process again. Profit-obsessed and bureaucracy-ridden, Hollywood, Bauer suggested, was incapable of carrying out worthy adaptations.

Assuming a stance contrary to hers, Gilbert Seldes argued in 1936 that adaptations *must* be "corrupt," and that they actually benefit from their corruption (3). He explained his notion of corruption by inventorying some of the ways in which a film may deviate from its source. It may, like *An American Tragedy,* carry a different message, or, like *Anatol,* a different atmosphere. The original's characters may be distorted, or its point twisted. What was once a tragedy may now be fitted with a happy ending (3). Seldes considered it axiomatic that an adaptation "cannot be a good reproduction of the original ... because the essence of the movie ... is movement; and the essential element in the originals is the word" (3). He compared the movement in films to the melody of a song:

> The actual words are of secondary importance (What we all remember of a film is, in nine cases out of ten, a movement and an action, sometimes supported by sound; rarely is it the spoken word or the theme. We do remember the plot, as it is expressed in action.) [4].

The "violence" done to originals is not willful, Seldes cautioned, but is the logical outcome of a need to hold films to a tolerable length (13). Thus, descriptions (save for visual) are rightly eliminated, as are minor episodes and characters, and dialog is pared to a vital minimum (13).

One of the questions Alice Evans Field sought to answer in her 1952 book *Hollywood, U.S.A.* is: "Why do motion picture producers make so many changes in filming a novel?" (46). She cited fellow analyst Frances Marion, who posited several likely reasons, to wit: Usually no more than a third of a novel represents action suitable for "picturization" (46). A screen narrative must move at a faster pace than do most novels; hence, anything extraneous to the plot must be omitted (47). On-screen events must be self-explanatory, or must be clarified by information made available in adjoining scenes (47). Whereas novels may have an overflow of characters and episodes—which must be cut for adaptation—they may conversely lack "acting situations," emotional content, and concreteness of character (47).

Summarizing the views of Marion and other film authorities, Field sorted narrative changes stemming from adaptation into three types:

1. Condensation, effected by choosing the most valued plot elements while discarding the rest;
2. Incorporation of additional scenes to close any gaps caused by condensation, or to fortify the drama; and
3. Modification of story components to bring the "moral tone" into conformance with the exacting standards of the industry's Production Code [51].

William Fadiman maintained strenuously in 1965 that to judge an adaptation purely as it relates to its source is "irresponsible" ("But Compared" 21). No film, he insisted, should be mistaken for a novel in celluloid guise. Cinema is, after all, a distinct medium, and "whether it improves or impairs the original material, it does so within its own conventions" (21). Doubting whether some critics grasped the meaning of the word "adaptation," he consulted a Webster's dictionary, the Producer-Writers' Guild Theatrical Basic Agreement, and the *World Film Encyclopedia*; in all three references he located language indicating that "adaptation" implies change, either for "new uses" or for "screen purposes" (22). On this basis, he concluded that to categorize a film as either a flawed imitation or an accurate reproduction of some other work is to ignore completely the theory, mechanics, and spirit of the medium (22).

Despite what some disgruntled critics may suspect, Fadiman lectured, Hollywood never purchases a novel simply to change it; no alterations are made out of "defiance or churlishness or quixotic caprice" ("But Compared" 23). One must remember that a novel is a peculiar, silent presentation, comprised solely of words; its messages are not meant to be heard or seen, but rather to be read (22).

Reinventing a fictional narrative for the screen is therefore not only morally permissible but logically inevitable. The instances of supposed "malpractice" perpetrated by adapters make for a daunting list: transforming a tragedy into a comedy or a farce; changing, deleting, or adding dialog; shifting nationalities, locales, and characters' ages; reversing genders; substituting reality for fantasy, and vice versa; disregarding authenticity; and generally engaging in flagrant license, intellectual and creative dishonesty, and deliberate debauchment and debasement of the original work (23). But, Fadiman reiterated, to belittle an adaptation on such grounds is imperceptive and unjust: a film must be judged *qua* film, irrespective of its origin.

Aligning himself with Fadiman, Lionel Godfrey supposed in 1967 that it would be "naive" not to expect some changes in an adaptation (12). What may succeed admirably in a novel may "have no chance at all" in a film, he wrote, so the quest for fidelity to the parent work is frankly "misguided" (12). In terms of drama, most novels are both "too diffuse and too restrained, ... seldom providing the bold stroke that can lead to striking images on the screen" (12). Film narratives must be comparatively visual and concentrated; here, Godfrey supplied the example of *Inside Daisy Clover*, with its nakedly emotional shots of the heroine (12–13). Sometimes, as in *Bel Ami*, adaptations become submerged in an artificial moralism, whereby sin is reliably punished by death (13). Often, a complicated structure must be simplified, or a limp one energized (14). On rare occasions, in dealing with a short story, such as Hemingway's "The Snows of Kilimanjaro," or a short novel, such as Walter Tevis' *The Hustler*, the adapter must bring about an expansion (14). "Until recently," Godfrey observed, "the 'positive' conclusion [to a film] was almost an invariable rule"—regardless of how the source might end (15). In all, fidelity, when it does occur, may result less from artistry than from timidity: from conservatism bent on garnering a mass audience (13).

In a contemporary article, D. T. Max outlines just what makes a novel attractive to Hollywood, with an emphasis on Scott Smith's *A Simple Plan*. Adaptable books are so scarce, Max states, that they cause producers to behave "like Russian shoppers," scrambling for whatever is available (130). To qualify as adaptable, a book must combine a viable premise, a clear story line, and strong roles for egotistical actors and actresses (130). Ostentatious prose and other trappings of high-flown literature are looked on with ambivalence. "Bad books sometimes make the best movies," allows Tom Pollock, Chairman of the MCA Motion Picture Group. "The best novels, with their textured characters, generally have to be radically rewritten" (Max 130). Minority protagonists, as in Terry McMillan's *Waiting to Exhale* and Amy Tan's *The Joy Luck Club*, also provoke uneasiness (130). As to Smith's *A Simple Plan*, its chief advantage may be its action-filled plot. "Things happen [in this story]," affirms literary agent Gail Hochman; "they're not just talked about or thought about" (Max 132).

SCHOLARLY POSITIONS

Probably the most significant film critic of the post–World War II era was André Bazin (Eberwein 71). In his essay "In Defense of Mixed Cinema," written circa 1950, Bazin noted glumly that the trend among adapters was to treat original materials with what he took as an unconscionable laxity. The writings of Dumas and Hugo were serving mainly to furnish filmmakers with "characters and adventures largely independent of their literary framework" (Bazin 53). Some characters, in fact, such as D'Artagnan and Javert, had become "part of a mythology existing outside the novels" (53). Bazin held the novel "more highly developed" than film (65), and capable of outperforming it in what many would consider the younger art's own province: subtle use of montage, reversal of chronology, and heightening of objectivity (64). Consequent to these opinions, he strongly urged faithful, though not quite slavish, adaptations. Fidelity, he understood, could be wrought through the creative use of equivalents: new language that may approximate some former meaning (67–68). He supposed, for example, that the omnipresent snow in Delannoy's *Symphonie pastorale* is a "moral coefficient" for André Gide's conspicuous simple past tenses (68).

In 1951 and 1952, Lester Asheim published a series of four articles on adaptation, all of them rooted in his 1949 doctoral dissertation. His observations sprang from a study of 24 novels and their film counterparts, including *David Copperfield*, *For Whom the Bell Tolls*, and *The Grapes of Wrath*. The first of these articles investigated Hollywood's tendency to simplify received narratives and highlighted several particulars: Asheim found that frequently the original dialog was tightened; the explicit was privileged over the implicit; lesser characters were dismissed; and some events were merged into each other or dropped outright ("Simplification" 294–301). His second article centered on three (still used) methods for achieving escapism and hence popular appeal; these involve compressing a universal problem into a personal difficulty, promoting a single character as the source of evil, and stressing the "sensational, exaggerated, and melodramatic" aspects of the core conflict while ignoring the more mundane ones ("Mass Appeals" 335–36). His third article analyzed Hollywood's habitual recourse to the love story and to the happy ending, which likewise operate on behalf of "nonrelevant escape" ("Affirmation" 54). If these features originated with the novel, they typically got magnified; if absent from the novel, they were apt to be invented (54–59).

Asheim set about, in his fourth article, to construct a grand overview of "adaptation technique[s] employed by the film industry when confronted with a novel of wide audience and high critical standing" ("Summary" 259). He was properly cautious, acknowledging the pitfalls of his slender sample and what in later years would become known as "overdetermination"—any one adaptive change may result from multiple causes (259). Still, he brought forth an extraordinary catalog of 39 principles, extending over six classifications, that affect how, what, and sometimes why adaptive changes are instituted. The classifications impinge on technology (a verbal approach must be converted into a visual one), artistry (plot is given more weight than character or philosophical nuance), audience limitations (a film audience is flatly assumed to have a lower level of comprehension than a literary audience), the star system (characters played by stars are given greater salience in the film than in the novel), societal pressures (violence and sex normally get reduced), and fidelity (the leading plot line is usually retained) ("Summary" 259–69).

Lavishly praised as "fascinating," "seminal," and "comprehensive," George Bluestone's *Novels into Film* is canonical to the scholarship of adaptation (McCaffrey 12; Huselberg 57; Kinney 18). This 1957 book divides, basically, into two sections: a lengthy introductory essay measuring the respective limits of the novel and the film, and then a sequence of case studies covering *Pride and Prejudice*, *The Ox-Bow Incident*, *Madame Bovary*, and other adaptations. It is primarily in the first section that the critic delineates the sharp, fundamental differences between the two media—differences that render a perfect correlation between any novel and any film based on it impossible.

Bluestone argued persuasively that fiction and film are as distinct as ballet and architecture (5). The two forms do intersect at the point of the shooting script, he admitted, but, once the film is completed, "they lose all resemblance to each other" (63). Indeed, the novel and the film reach out to us with separate histories (6–14), raw materials (14–31), felt influences (31–45), and psychological appeals (45–61). As such, statements along the lines of "The film is true to the spirit of the book" and "It's incredible how they butchered the novel" are predicated on false assumptions: that novels have a

> separable content which may be detached and reproduced, as the snapshot reproduces the kitten; that incidents and characters in fiction are interchangeable with incidents and characters in the film; that the novel is a norm and the film deviates at its peril; that ... the extent of the deviation will vary directly with the "respect" one has for the original... [5].

It is more valid to assume that what the filmmaker adapts is a "kind of paraphrase of the novel" (62). That is, he or she does not view the source as a novel per se, but as a collection of characters and incidents that have "somehow detached themselves from language and, like the heroes of folk legends, have achieved a mythic life of their own" (62). (Of course, the same thought occurred to Bazin, but less congenially.) In effect, Bluestone concluded, the adapter is not so much a translator as a new author (62).

Donald McCaffrey agreed, in 1967, that the novel and the film are demarked from each other, and are comparable only to a limited degree (11). On this basis, he wondered why so many adapted films follow the structural pattern of their models. He granted that overt fidelity soothes the public, and that some faithful adaptations—*The House of the Seven Gables, Little Women, Captains Courageous*—have been competently, if slickly, produced (12). Yet he saw little sign of "artistry" or "greatness" in these films (12). The problem, as he construed it, is that a novel may range readily over a wide variety of actions and still find unity in its theme. By contrast, a film seems less able to prosper with a far-flung or episodic structure; it requires unity of action, not just of theme (14–15). Depending on the kind of novel utilized as a source, the faithful adapter, hoping to please a perspicacious audience, may actually be inviting failure. With its concentrated dramatic presence, film, McCaffrey thought, "cannot handle the breadth of the epic novel without sacrificing ... effectiveness" (17).

Asserting that "most" films are adapted (1), Jean Mitry discussed in 1971 what he considered the central problem of adaptation. Different means of expression, he suggested, necessarily "express different things—not the same things in different ways" (1). To speak, then, of adaptation as if it were a matter of translation, a passing from one language to another, is erroneous; adaptation is a "passing from one *form* to another, a matter of transposition, of reconstruction" (1). Every adapter is faced with two options: he or she may strive to be faithful to the letter of the original, following the "procedure of the novelist step-by-step so that the chains of circumstance are exactly the same"; or, conversely, he or she may be faithful to its spirit, arriving, via slanted routes, at ideas and situations analogous to those already encountered (4). In his view, either option has its drawbacks. The first leads to unimaginative work that, despite benevolent intentions, distorts the original; the second, to a distortion equally profound, since "to betray the letter [of the source] is to betray the spirit" *ipso facto*—according to Mitry, the spirit lives nowhere but in the letter (4). To his mind, any victory the adapter wins is Pyrrhic.

Writing his 1973 tome *The Impact of Film*, Roy Paul Madsen proposed that any similarities between the novel and the film are superficial. In reality, he stated, the two are as different as "music and sculpture" (254). (One notices that Madsen's opening comments on the adaptation of novels [253–54] echo Bluestone's almost identically, though he gives his benefactor no credit.) He then reviewed a host of concerns that the adapter must keep in mind if a changeover is to succeed. Among them are media disparities (the novel is verbal; the film, visual); suitability for adaptation (an introspective literary style presents tougher obstacles); condensation (film is less able to manage a sprawling scope); point of view (films are usually narrated in the third person, despite how the novel may be narrated); equivalence (cinematic devices must often be substituted for literary ones); leading characters (roles may be altered to meet the needs or demands of a star performer); dialog (speech must be natural, not poetic); taste (films, especially those intended for an American audience, tend to conclude on an uplifting—not on a frustrating—note); and universal issues (good and evil are likely to be personified) (254–63).

Charles Eidsvik posited in 1975 that expectations affect how the public reacts to films, and especially to adaptations (255). If a non-adapted film contains just 20 enjoyable minutes, the viewer considers these minutes a treat and is "willing to put up with a lot during the other hour or two that the film runs" (255). But in the case of an adaptation, one's presumed familiarity with the original work imposes terribly high expectations that may cause him or her to feel "betrayed" or "cheated" by the film (255). Even its worthwhile moments may slip by unappreciated. Eidsvik submitted that this sort of intolerance is wrongheaded, if only because adaptations dependably offer "major advances in the art of film" (255). Beset by adaptive quandaries, filmmakers are stimulated to reach innovative solutions that, by chance, may profitably expose hallowed cinematic terms for the "clichéd conventions" they might be (256). Then too, sometimes the solutions usher in brand-new cinematic terms. Sometimes they succeed for "no known reason at all" (256).

With some eccentricity, Eidsvik went on to adduce four reasons adaptations are beneficial to literature, and five reasons they are beneficial to film. Taking up their salutary effects on literature, he averred that films function as introductions to books; they "help get books out of college classrooms and into the streets"; they act to restore literature's links with its popular, melodramatic past; and they incite fiction writers, who dislike being co-opted, to become more aggressively experimental (258–59). As to positive impacts on film, adaptations are an impetus for striking deals; they represent, through the original works, a potent source of raw material; they enable Hollywood to assuage the middle class by reducing "dangerous books" to consumer romance; they present filmmakers with interesting technical challenges; and they keep Hollywood in touch, however distantly, with lofty intellectual standards (259–60).

In distinguishing between film and literature, Bernard Dick concomitantly threw light on the problem of adaptation. Film, he wrote in 1978, does at times draw on literature, and, like opera librettos, might be classified as one of its branches (73). Yet film, he alleged, differs from literature in at least four ways:

1. In film, the laws of verisimilitude are more often relaxed [73]. Ingmar Bergman's *Wild Strawberries*, for example, begins with Isak's prolog describing his journey to Stockholm, an adventure that seems to be a "death trip" [73]. But if Isak dies, how is he able to narrate his retrospective prolog?
2. The visual, in film, takes priority over the verbal [73]. Again, in *Wild Strawberries*, images redolent of death—a coffin, a clock without hands, a car that resembles a hearse—overpower words, so that the viewer comes to accept the troubling prolog as simply "a way of beginning the film" [73].
3. Mythic associations are more readily implied in film [73]. In their purest form, Dick avowed, myths are pictures— "autonomous, numinous, and self-taught" [74]; films are therefore better designed to accommodate them.
4. The authorship of a film is virtually always multiple [74]. Whereas the novel *The Last Tycoon* was authored solely by Fitzgerald, the 1976 film version absorbed his influence, but also that of screenwriter Harold Pinter and director Elia Kazan. Dick sensed that Pinter's contribution might actually be dominant—the parataxis and disconnectedness that characterize the film's dialog belong plainly to him [75].

In 1982, Donald Larsson made a preliminary attempt, from a Marxist perspective, to devise a framework within which adaptations may be more clearly understood (69). What scholarship needs, he contended, is a "*theory* of adaptations"; such a theory would perforce be alert to the history of adaptive motivations and techniques and to the methods of recoding fiction for the screen (69). He held that adaptation too regularly impoverishes the original narrative, and that the reasons for this impoverishment may be descried in three areas: the historical matrix of the novel, the aesthetic intent of the adapter, and the ideological constraints that shepherd a text toward moral and political conformity (71). As one becomes distanced from a novel in time, cultural changes may make certain of its aspects seem antiquated, hence disposable (72). Moreover, some popular novels become widely enshrined as "Acceptable Literature," their rough edges pointedly forgotten (73). As to aesthetics, adapters, sensitive to profits, have traditionally been more faithful to the original than to themselves; this (misplaced) fidelity has led to a paucity of radical adaptations (75–78). Finally, artworks engendered under the sway of a given ideology typically reproduce that ideology—and so it is with novels and films (79).

    The nub of research into adaptation, Dudley Andrew wrote in 1984, is the "matching of the cinematic sign system to prior achievement in some other system" (96). By so doing, one discovers that the modes of relationship between the adapted film and the prior text are three, which Andrew labeled "borrowing," "intersection," and "fidelity of transformation" (98). Borrowing is probably the most common mode, and involves taking just a grain of material—an idea, a structure, an afflatus—from an earlier, well-known text (98). Here, the audience is "expected to enjoy basking in a certain pre-established presence and to call up new or especially powerful aspects of a cherished work" (98); an example would be Strauss' adaptation of Cervantes' *Don Quixote* (98). At the opposite end of the spectrum lies intersection, in which the integrity of the original is almost entirely preserved despite adaptation; an instance, also mentioned by Bazin (68), is Robert Bresson's version of Georges Bernanos' *Diary of a Country Priest* (Andrew 99). Then there is fidelity of transformation, to be found in some hazy hinterland between the extremes: the adapter hopes to abstract "something essential" from the original, and to carry that vital ingredient across the vale to the new medium (100). Deceptively subtle, this third mode has aroused the most debate (101).

Practical Positions

A pioneer of adaptation and a champion of strict fidelity, director Allan Dwan, in 1919, outlined his mission thus:

> To take the theme, swing of the story, situations and characters from the author's pages and transfer them to the screen so that you, remembering the story, would be pleased, and so that you, never having chanced to read it, would be pleased—briefly, holding old friends and making new friends for the tale [299].

In pursuit of these goals, he adhered to a number of rules. He avoided stars, since yielding to their whims might undermine a story's "original charm" (299). He gave inordinate attention to the characters, aspiring to know them thoroughly before even thinking of prospective actors and actresses (299). He was sensitive to visual details, minding "beauty of background, ... beauty of photographic effects, ... accuracy of costume and of locale..." (301). The tone of the story was also important to him, and he favored those with "clean and decent American characters, clean, courageous, bold, adventurous men and plucky, charming women" (303). He saw merit in poetic justice and in the happy ending (303). Above all, he believed in rollicking action—"for action is what makes the most popular photoplays" (304). Dwan worried that the adaptation of novels and plays puts Hollywood in a "parasitical state" (304), and he correctly predicted the rise of non-adapted screenplays (305).

Screenwriter-producer Jerry Wald, who contributed to such adaptations as *Brother Rat*, *Key Largo*, and *Picnic*, called film, in 1954, a genuine "art form," and asserted that some screenwriters are as masterful in their field as Thomas Mann and Somerset Maugham were in theirs (63). At the same time, he lamented the anonymity to which screenwriters are consigned, and the frustrations they must endure in attempting adaptations (62). Drawing on assorted mythologies, he compared reworking a celebrated novel or play first to living in a purgatory, and then to steering a delicate, perilous course between the "Scylla of the [initial] author and the Charybdis of the public" (62). Still, if the adapter is sufficiently skilled and conscientious, he or she may "perform a service to the motion picture and to literature itself" (63). To do so requires the proper attitude, as Wald's colleague David Taradash, who adapted *From Here to Eternity*, explained:

> The matter of responsibility in adapting a fine novel is ... mostly a matter of respect for the material. That is, for the heart of the material, for what you feel the author tried to say.... You have to be bold in breaking away from the book when it becomes necessary. But there are certain key scenes, and definite aspects of character, which have to be retained....
>
> The business of adapting a novel is something like the business of being a parent. You have to be stern with the child but you have to love him constantly and be aware that your function is to cater to his needs and not vice versa [Wald 64].

Wald isolated two significant challenges that the adapter must meet: controlling the length of the script, and recognizing what must be changed (64). He or she must locate the chief characters, the central theme, and the best dialog in order to deliver a story of "sittable" duration—preferably no more than 120 minutes (64). In determining what to cut, the adapter must rely on "taste, tact, and judgment" (65). The hope is always to retain the thrust and flavor of the original, yet this end may be striven for only within the claustrophobic confines of a severe artistic economy (66). "The novelist," Wald preached, "can have an army of elephants move through the Alps into Italy.... The screenwriter must find ways of *suggesting* the same incident" (emphasis added) (66).

Recalling his own labors in Hollywood, DeWitt Bodeen proposed in 1963 to impart an "idea of what a writer goes through in adapting a well-known property to the screen" (349). At different times, Bodeen was contracted to write the (adaptive) screenplays for *The Enchanted Cottage*, originally a play by Arthur Wing Pinero; *I Remember Mama*, based on a collection of short stories by Kathryn Forbes; and *Billy Budd*, from Melville's famous novella. In reimagining *The Enchanted Cottage*, which he described as a muddle of "sentimentality and clumsy dream sequences," Bodeen jettisoned everything but the rudiments of the main story line before rebuilding (350). With the second assignment, he struggled to decide which of the individual stories should be integrated into the master narrative; in the end, he fragmented one, and was forced to discard some others (352). Arriving at *Billy Budd*, he ruminated on the secret, mystical, and "even obtuse" meanings lurking in the tale, before choosing the "most dramatic" slant (356). Bodeen confided that writing an original screenplay is comparatively refreshing: "imagination can do ... as it will; one is free" (356). But writing an adaptation asks for "selective interpretation, along with an ability to recreate and sustain an established mood"—a much more trying task (356).

One of Hollywood's most accomplished screenwriters is William Goldman; among his numerous credits are *All the President's Men*, *Marathon Man*, and *Misery*—all adaptations. In his 1983 book *Adventures in the Screen Trade*, he shared two insights he feels every screenwriter should keep in mind. First, "SCREENPLAYS ARE STRUCTURE" (*sic*), meaning that screenplays—including those that are drawn from a prior work—have a greater dependency on an uncompromised architecture than do most other types of creative writing (195). Sparkling dialog is desirable, he conceded, as are convincing characters, but "if the structure is unsound, forget it" (195). Second, every narrative has a "spine," the "absolutely crucial" element that affords the piece its specialness (196). The adapter must locate and protect the spine "to the death" (196). Further, Goldman advised that he or she be able to answer correctly a series of questions: What is the story about? On a deeper, more intimate plane, what is the story really about? What must be done regarding time—the time *of* the story and the time *in* it? Who tells the story? Where does it take place? What adjustments must be made with respect to the characters? Finally, what must be preserved (312–24)?

In their 1988 manual on scriptwriting, Dwight Swain and Joye Swain examined three possible means of adapting a novel. First, the adapter can follow the pattern of the book closely; this method is fraught with difficulties since a novel is likely to feature more characters than a film can gracefully accept, a more intricate design, and more plentiful climaxes (196). The only solution to the disharmony, they wrote, is to cut vigorously, but of course the solution itself subverts the implied wish for strong fidelity (196). Second, the adapter can work from key scenes—those that seem colorful, dramatic, and indicative of the author's concept (196). The chosen scenes are arranged into a climactic order and bridged together with either new or residual materials. Third, the adapter can develop what amounts to an "original" screenplay, influenced only faintly by the book (197). This scheme calls for him or her to retain the story's underlying premise, but then to abandon inconvenient details as necessity dictates and fancy allows (197). None of these alternatives is infallible, but the authors cautioned that excessive fidelity may yield a script that "never quite jells: a straggly thing replete with loose ends, abortive scenes, jerky development, and characters who never quicken" (200).

Kubrick's Position

If a pluralist would take the foregoing views as approximately equal in value, an Orwellian might object that some views are more equal than others. Anticipating this hypothetical objection, I present Stanley Kubrick's views separately, since, in this context, his may be the most equal of all.

Like his films, Kubrick's beliefs about adaptation appear to have been carefully reasoned; like his films, they are somewhat unconventional. He professes that the novel he considers most adaptable is not one of action but, to the contrary, one that is concerned with the "inner life of its characters" (Kubrick 306). Such a novel supposedly endows him with an "absolute compass bearing, as it were, on what a character is thinking or feeling at any given moment" (306). The advantage here is that he is necessarily spurred to invent actions—objective correlatives—that reflect the novel's psychological drift; the characters' thoughts and emotions are thereby demonstrated, not baldly declared. In this connection, if a film's revelations about life are to be meaningful, they must be advanced obliquely, so that the audience is permitted the "thrill in making the discovery" of the truth (306).

Kubrick believes that "almost every novel can be successfully adapted, provided it is not one whose artistic integrity is lost along with its length" (306–7). A novel that might offer resistance, then, is one with an abundance of variform action, all of which is indispensable to the story (307). He is unintimidated by the putatively great novel, such as *Lolita*. Great novels, like mediocre ones, may be adapted, though the results, even if competent, are more subject to heavy criticism (306). Kubrick notes that much of what contributes to the great novel's aura is its style, a quality he suspects is misunderstood. He defines style as "what an artist uses to fascinate the beholder in order to convey … his [or her] feelings and emotions and thoughts" (307). In fact, it is this set of unseen obsessions that gets dramatized, he insists, and not style.

The screenwriter engaged in adaptation must realize that he or she works not so much with "paper and ink and words" as with "flesh and feeling" (Kubrick 308). Too few writers, Kubrick notices, have a sense of what an actor can and cannot communicate emotionally. Sometimes a poorly written script indicates unrealistically that a silent look is to transmit some multilayered message; on other occasions, "the actor is given a long speech to convey something that is quite apparent in the situation" (308). Kubrick exhorts writers to envisage actors not as anarchists who might ruin a script, but as an integral part of the film world (308). Going further, he declares that directing is nothing more or less than a "continuation of the writing," and that the screenwriter-director, through virtuosity, is the ideal dramatic (and adaptive) instrument (308).

A sagacious adapter, Kubrick explains, seeks out and negotiates the *via media*. To start, he or she should be "one hundred percent faithful to the author's meaning and … sacrifice none of it for the sake of climax or effect" (Kubrick 308). Disregarding the material's "inner design" often leads to a superficial product that may excite in the short term but then abruptly fizzle (308). On the other hand, one must not be overly rigid. Allowing the work to grow through collaboration—through a dedicated "to-and-fro" among the script, director, and actors—tends not only to improve the project but to elate the participants (309).

Although Kubrick, as an inveterate adapter, has been attracted to a variety of stories, he perceives certain commonalties among them:

> I have always enjoyed dealing with a slightly surrealistic situation and presenting it in a realistic manner. I've always liked fairy tales and myths, magical stories, supernatural stories, ghost stories, surrealistic and allegorical stories. I think they are somehow closer to the sense of reality one feels today than the equally stylized "realistic" story in which a great deal of selectivity and omission has to occur in order to preserve its "realistic" style [Houston 44].

From his vantage, all the stories to which he has turned are charged with a "passionate sense of truth" (Reynolds 144). Kubrick maintains that, in the last analysis, he would never film a story that he is not "finally in love with" (Houston 44).

Approach and Method

As I mentioned at the outset, my approach to the problem of adaptation is rhetorical. Aristotle defined rhetoric as the "faculty of observing in any given case the available means of persuasion" (24), and it is fair to state that the term's nuclear meaning has changed little since his day. What has changed is the array of subjects to which the term is applied. Traditionally, rhetoric has been associated almost exclusively with formal, spoken address; but in recent decades scholars have acknowledged the rhetoric of "essays, conversations, poetry, novels, stories, television programs, films, art, architecture, plays, music, dance, advertisements, furniture, public demonstrations, and dress" (Foss 4). Further complicating matters is the commonly accepted division of rhetorical criticism into formalist and ideological camps (Lehman 4; Hart 381–422). The first includes those who would (benignly) examine a rhetorical object's structural attributes; the second, those who would explore (perhaps not so benignly) the object's political content, or how the object is used politically by society. So to announce with no added elucidation that one has opted to undertake a rhetorical study is, as Donald Bryant jocosely puts it, "potentially to step off into a pretty soggy morass—there to conjure with confusion, amble in ambiguity, [and] manipulate misconception" (3).

My own brand of rhetorical criticism is formalist, and has been influenced by several individual critics and by at least three sweeping intellectual movements. From the ranks of critics, I would name Wayne Booth, Thomas Benson and Carolyn Anderson, and James Andrews. Regarding the movements, I would point to New Criticism, neoformalism, and humanism. By commenting on these influences as I will herewith, and especially by homing in on what I admire in them, I believe I can clarify some of my own values and critical guideposts.

Wayne Booth, whose 1961 treatise *The Rhetoric of Fiction* is now judged something of a landmark, was among the first to hold that fiction may and should be seen through a rhetorical template. The subject of his book is the panoply of "rhetorical resources available to the writer of epic, novel, or short story as he [or she] tries, consciously or unconsciously, to impose [a] fictional world upon the reader" (xiii). (One notes immediately that the fictional world does not exist for its own sake, but instead to be "imposed" on others in an act of communication.) Some of the questions Booth raises are: How can an author ensure that dramatic moments are heightened rather than obscured by their surroundings? How can an author achieve dramatic irony, or suspense? How can an author prevent a sentimental reading of this character, or a hostile reading of that one (64)? Obviously the answers to these questions vary according to circumstance, but always they involve the utilization of rhetoric.

Introducing *Reality Fictions: The Films of Frederick Wiseman*, Thomas Benson and Carolyn Anderson set forth their philosophy of film analysis:

> Films are social constructions and as such invite shared experiences. The rhetorical critic inquires into that shared experience, not by surveying audience response, and not simply by reporting the critic's subjective, impressionistic responses, but by interrogating the film itself, regarding the film as a constructed invitation to a complex experience of thoughts and feelings.... Properly executed, ... a rhetorical criticism, in identifying both the experience of the

film and the way in which the film brings about that experience, may open the film to discussion.... Part of the ethical obligation of the rhetorical critic is to attempt to persuade viewers, on occasion, how they should view a film [2–3].

I find the tenor of these comments appealing, and would add that they strike me as applicable to novels as well.

James Andrews' credo of rhetorical criticism is likewise affirmative in tone. He recalls John Dewey's observation that criticism "is not fault-finding.... It is judgment engaged in discriminating among values. It is taking thought as to what is better and worse in any field at any time, with some consciousness of *why* the worse is worse" (3–4). For his part, Andrews frames criticism as a "process of illumination and evaluation" that hands down "ultimate pronouncements" only with caution (4). The critic's objective is not to destroy, but to build understanding: a "fuller and richer understanding of a particular work as it exists within the context of human endeavor" (4). The rendering of "certain judgments," either approving or disapproving, is not inappropriate, but the critic is, in the end, less an arbiter than an "educator" (6).

The term "New Criticism" became widely recognized and accepted in the 1940s, following the publication of John Crowe Ransom's eponymously titled collection of essays (Sutton 99). But the movement itself had its origins in critical works published by I. A. Richards and T. S. Eliot in the 1920s and 1930s (Sutton 99–100). Along with these luminaries, some of the better known practitioners were Cleanth Brooks, Allen Tate, and R. P. Blackmur. By 1960 the movement had largely dissipated (Sutton 98), though even today its ghostly, lingering presence is still felt by not only literary but film critics. As David Bordwell (with undisguised ruefulness) grants: "Whatever school, trend, or movement to which a critic pledges allegiance, the practice of interpreting a text proceeds along lines laid down by New Criticism" (23).

The New Critics propounded a wealth of ideas about literature and criticism, some of which I find more congenial than others. I do not believe, as did Eliot, that a particular work may reasonably represent the artist's "talking to himself—or to nobody" ("Three Voices" 89); the artist is, for better or worse, in contact with an audience. Nor do I think that recourse to an artist's biography or stated intentions is necessarily misdirected, as did Brooks (Sutton 116). I harbor no special antipathy toward science, as did Ransom, who stamped its knowledge "ruthless and exclusive" (Ransom 140). On the other side, I do have a high esteem for Eliot's concept of a historic "tradition" ("Individual Talent" 49–51). Anticipating the neoformalist awareness of "backgrounds," he writes: "No artist has ... complete meaning alone" (49). The perception that form and meaning are bound up in each other—that "all the elements [of an artwork] are vitally interfused"—is fundamentally rhetorical (Brooks and Warren 341). And like the New Critics, I appreciate the value of a "close reading," a detailed and subtle analysis of the interrelations and ambiguities within a text.

Neoformalism reaches back to the perspective of the Russian Formalist literary critics. Prominent in Russia from about 1915 to 1930, they included Vladimir Propp, Viktor Shklovsky, Roman Jakobson, and Boris Eichenbaum. Neoformalism is essentially the contemporary application of Russian Formalism to the analysis of film and, to a lesser degree, other kinds of art (Thompson 5–6). The school cleaves to several principles, of which these are foundational:

1. Art exists separately from other cultural phenomena; assessing it responsibly asks for a specialized, aesthetic, non-practical perceptiveness (Thompson 8).
2. All art involves "defamiliarization" by the artist and by the critic (Thompson 10–11). The artist, as Shklovsky writes, tries to "impart the sensation of things as they are perceived, and not as they are known" (qtd. in Thompson 10). Similarly, the critic must strive to apprehend this freshness.
3. A film may be explored through its devices. A device is any single element or structure that plays a role in the artwork—a camera movement, a repeated word, a theme (Thompson 15). In theory, a device always has a function (15).
4. Films should be considered in the context of history: in relation to other artworks and to everyday experience. The norms of prior experience are called "backgrounds" (Thompson 21). Whether a film conforms to, or deviates from, a given background suggests how viewers will respond (21).

All these tenets seem sensible to me; I disagree with none of them.

My approach, finally, is suffused with a modest dose of humanism. The humanist critic is inclined to mull over his or her personal encounter with a work, to draw conclusions about the value of that encounter, and then to pass the conclusions along to others (Bywater and Sobchack 25). Having viewed a film, a humanist might raise the following questions: What does it reveal about the human condition? How do form and content interact to generate the film's meaning? Is there an artist behind the film? How does it rate in comparison with others (25–26)? Tim Bywater and Thomas Sobchack enlarge on this train:

> The humanist looks for representations in film of general human values, the truths of human experience as they relate to the common and universal aspects of human existence—birth, death, love, aggression, happiness, sorrow—seeking the answer to the question: "What is there in this film or in my experience of it that will help me understand the variety and complexity of the human heart and mind?" [27].

My method—and like Thompson (6–7), I use the word to signify a specific procedure, as opposed to the more open-ended "approach"—calls for discrete, analytical discussions of three films and their fictional progenitors. The films I have selected were extensively publicized, critiqued, and debated. Moreover, though directed by the same person, they offer the critical virtue of being very different from each other. *Lolita* is a perverse love story; *The Shining* a horror story; and *Full Metal Jacket* a war story. One surmises, therefore, that any adaptive trends the three may share are robust and worth contemplating.

Following some brief, prefatory remarks, each of my discussions will look first to a short section of the film, then backward to the corresponding passage, or passages, in the novel. This cycle will then repeat until the discussion is concluded. Generally, my concern will go to changes in the story, and to the effects these changes bring about; where it seems appropriate, I will also comment on what does not change. As befits the rhetorical critic, I intend to describe, to interpret, and, here and there, to evaluate (Brock, Scott, and Chesebro 16). In the process, I hope to shine new light on the works under scrutiny, and on the venerable problem of adaptation.

Chapter 2
Lolita

Vladimir Nabokov's twelfth novel *Lolita* is styled as the confessions of one "Humbert Humbert"—he hides behind a pseudonym—who, nearing middle age, becomes sexually involved with a pubescent girl, Dolores Haze, or Lolita. (During the course of their dalliance, he ages from 37 to 39; she from 12 to 14.) A European-born intellectual, Humbert has long been fascinated by "nymphets," certain girls between the ages of nine and 14 whose allure, to his taste, is irresistible. In the New England town of Ramsdale, he encounters his pluperfect nymphet in Lolita, and marries her mother solely to keep access to the child. When the mother, Charlotte, dies in a car accident, he looks eagerly forward to abusing his stepdaughter in her sleep. This unseemliness is obviated, however, when Lolita actually seduces Humbert, transcending his fantasies. The two then depart on an odyssey that takes them around the country, ending in Beardsley, where she attends school and falls under the spell of another pedophile, Clare Quilty. Humbert and Lolita embark on a second motel-dotted journey, but Quilty pursues them, and eventually steals Lolita away. Some three years later, Humbert reencounters her, now destitute, pregnant, and married to a Richard Schiller. When she declines to rejoin Humbert, he tearfully gives her money and sets out after Quilty, whom he kills. Both Humbert and Lolita soon follow in death.

The outré subject matter led to what Riley Hughes has laconically characterized as the novel's "somewhat sensational [early] career" (72). Completed in 1954, the manuscript was rejected by four American publishers, whose readers were purportedly "shocked"

(Nabokov, "On a Book" 314–15). It was finally published a year later in Paris by Maurice Girodias' Olympia Press, a house affiliated with the "infamous Travellers Companion series, the green-backed books once so familiar and dear to the eagle-eyed inspectors of the U. S. Customs" (Appel xxxiii). In short order, *Lolita* was banned by Austria, England, Burma, Belgium, and Australia (Golson 62); the French government, in its turn, forbade the book's export (Hicks 12). It was not until 1958 that Putnam, fortified by an array of critical hosannas, brought out an American edition (Appel xxxv). In 1964, *Playboy* reported that *Lolita*, having thrived on the controversy, had sold 2.5 million copies in the United States alone (Golson 62).

From the standpoint of adaptation, the novel's notoriety was probably a mixed blessing. As the object of a sustained critical "uproar" (Hicks 12), *Lolita* burst brightly and loudly upon the public's awareness and quickly became a best-seller—a rarity for any book so challengingly erudite (Meyer 340). Yet the very quality that contributed to its popularity, its air of debased eroticism, must have made *Lolita* seem a dubious project in Hollywood. Indeed, Alexander Walker suggests that one reason Kubrick shot the film version in England was the lowered risk of harassment from pressure groups (*Sex in the Movies* 171). As the film was readied for release, so many people were flabbergasted at the news that Nabokov's novel had been adapted into a socially acceptable film that the question "How did they ever make a movie of *Lolita*?" became an advertising tag line (Crowther 23).

Aside from its outlandish content and reputation, the novel possesses at least two other features that militated against its being adapted: its signal style and its labyrinthine complexity. (In *Lolita* and throughout Nabokov's work these attributes tend to coil around each other.) Walter Allen wrote that *Lolita* is "told with sparkling brilliance" (632); Conrad Brenner applauded a prose that is "flamboyant, free, liberated; conceived in joy" (20); and Thomas Molnar rhapsodized at length:

> Mr. Nabokov's English is beautiful and immensely suggestive, espousing with the greatest ease the mood of men, the color of landscapes, the ambiance of motels, girls' schools, and small towns.

It is an ocean of a language, now calm, limpid, transparent, then turning into a roar, with waves upon waves of scintillating metaphors, images, innovations, allusions. The author swims in this ocean like a smooth-bodied fish, leaving the pursuer-reader amidst a thousand delights [102].

The book's complexity stems not just from the mere quantity of its parts, but from the subtle and devious relations among them. As Appel observes, *Lolita* is an "involuted" work, full of elaborate tricks that simultaneously mock and expand the traditional notion of fiction (xix–xxxiii). Exquisite literature, it was no doubt avoided, if one can have faith in Tom Pollock's remarks, by more than a few filmmakers (Max 130).

But Kubrick, who believes that "almost any novel" can be satisfactorily adapted (Kubrick 306), was undeterred by these potential problem areas. Certainly his blanket optimism meant that he would not refuse the project preemptively. It might also be recognized, however, that Nabokov's *Lolita* is not wholly lacking in values that could attract a commercial filmmaker, and Kubrick especially. It contains, for example, more than its share of physical (nonsexual) action: kaleidoscopic travel, weird confrontations, a fatal accident, a grotesque murder. It is designed to pull not only at the cortex but at the heart; Elizabeth Janeway labeled it as both one of the funniest and saddest novels she had ever read (5). The characters are drawn vividly, and the two main ones find, after their sordid misconduct, a touch of redemption in the end. With his stated predilections, Kubrick could not have helped noticing the story's occasional glint of surrealism, and the detailed if roily inner life of the first-person narrator.

Reviews of the film ranged in tone from unmitigated approval to mild disappointment. Those who liked the film had particular kudos for the direction. Phillip Hartung submitted that Kubrick got the best from his performers (401); Hollis Alpert compared Kubrick favorably to Orson Welles (40); and Paul Beckley called Kubrick's "style and treatment and timing and eye for the telling detail a continual cinematic delight" (16). Many of those critics who had reservations complained that the story, transformed, loses too much of its wicked edge. *Variety* likened the film to a bee without its stinger

("Lolita" 6); Dwight MacDonald brooded that the "erotic and perverse flavor" of the novel has been largely expunged (45); and *Time*'s reviewer groused that the original's shades of meaning have been "filtered out" ("Humbert Humdrum" 94). For his part, Nabokov viewed the film with an approbation that seems gradually to have lessened. "I thought the movie was absolutely first-rate," he said in 1964 (Golson 63). But nine years later he admitted:

> My first reaction to the picture was a mixture of aggravation, regret, and reluctant pleasure. Quite a few of the extraneous inventions (such as the macabre ping-pong scene or that rapturous swig of Scotch in the bathtub) struck me as appropriate and delightful. Others (such as the collapsing cot or the frills of Miss Lyon's elaborate nightgown) were painful [Nabokov, *A Screenplay* xiii].

As with the films I analyze in Chapters 3 and 4, I have sectioned *Lolita* into manageable portions according to its structure. Within this scheme, not every change, and not every constancy, is noted—there are thousands of each. But with some deference to Herbert Wichelns, I attempt to isolate those items that yield what I perceive as the greatest effects.

Prelude

Filmed in black-and-white, Kubrick's *Lolita* begins with a tableau. As lush, orchestral music plays and the opening credits materialize and vanish, a bare, dainty foot appears against a satiny backdrop. Off-center, the name "Lolita" is superimposed over the foot, identifying its owner as well as the film. A man's left hand immediately accepts the foot, cradling it, while his right hand now inserts a tuft of cotton between the first and second toe. With a tiny brush, he lovingly paints the first nail. The process continues: A second tuft is inserted, and the second toe is delicately daubed. When the final credit—a reference to Stanley Kubrick as director—fades, the last toe receives a single stroke, and the scene concludes.

One would search the novel in vain for a double to the sequence described; it was invented for the film. Its function is to set the tone of the narrative, and, even more, to capture one aspect of the intemperate relationship between the man—Humbert—and Lolita. We note that he is much larger and apparently much stronger than she, but the worshipful care he lavishes upon her argues that the true locus of power lies with Lolita. As Peter Bunzel observed, Humbert undertakes the pedicure with "such absorption that there is no mistaking either his adoration or his pathetic enslavement" (97). In fact, the first paragraph of the novel's first chapter urges the same impression, though in different terms. Humbert begins by expressing his enthrallment for the girl and, like a schoolboy, for her very name:

> Lolita, light of my life, fire of my loins. My sin, my soul. Lo-lee-ta: the tip of the tongue taking a trip of three steps down the palate to tap, at three, on the teeth. Lo. Lee. Ta [*Lolita* 11].

Here, the film has made a verbal message richly visual.

Kubrick's decision to shoot in black-and-white also bears comment, since the tactic seems to be at odds with Nabokov's pavonine prose. The writer's language is colorful in two senses: in its bracing resourcefulness and unpredictability, and in its frequent references to assorted hues. Consider these snatches of description, as Humbert recalls his and Lolita's first venture across the country:

> Beyond the tilled plain, beyond the toy roofs, there would be a slow suffusion of inutile loveliness, a low sun in a platinum haze with a warm, peeled-peach tinge pervading the upper edge of a two-dimensional, dove-gray cloud fusing with the distant amorous mist.... Or again, [the scene] might be a stern El Greco horizon, pregnant with inky rain, ... and all around alternating strips of quick-silverish water and harsh green corn [*Lolita* 154–55].

By opting for black-and-white, Kubrick quells these glories and many others, bringing the film the grainy aspect of a documentary. Under the circumstances—a risqué topic, zealous censors—his restraint seems to have been a calculated and conservative move.

After the toe-painting scene, we watch Humbert drive through a fog to the palatial home of Clare Quilty. In his handsome, mouton-collar coat, Humbert enters the residence and finds himself in a kind of wasteland, emblematic of Quilty's soul—the floor is littered with bottles, glasses, statues, sheet-covered furniture, even a harp. A drunken Quilty eventually reveals himself, and, intimidated by his purposeful visitor, tries bizarrely to engage him in a game of Ping-Pong. Quilty seems not to remember Humbert, and acknowledges only a dim remembrance of Lolita. Humbert produces a gun and informs Quilty that he, Quilty, is about to die; Quilty responds with jokes and non sequiturs. Humbert now has him read some verse intended to explain Quilty's fate. Still tetched, or pretending to be, Quilty dons boxing gloves, takes them off in the wake of a tentative gunshot, and, babbling nervously, plays his piano. When he finally makes a dash to escape, Humbert fires several shots at him, one of which wounds his leg. Humbert coolly reloads his revolver and shoots repeatedly at his quarry, who takes ineffectual cover behind a painting of a young girl.

The most obvious difference between this scene and its fictional analog is the position it occupies in the narrative. In the book, the killing of Quilty occurs soon after Humbert's last conversation with Lolita in Coalmont. Its function is climactic and purgative, and the scant action that takes place afterward is, as Humbert puts it, "flattish and faded" (*Lolita* 307): he drives away, is caught, and takes a moment to regret his sins. But appearing at the start of the film, Quilty's execution acts both as an outcome—we instantly flash backward four years—and as an introduction. Readers of the novel learn in the first chapter that Humbert is a murderer; viewers of the film likewise receive this information early. In addition, the film's unorthodox opening creates a curiosity about Humbert's motivation in committing murder, thereby carrying the audience, in theory at least, beyond "what will happen when he and Lolita hit the next motel" (Bunzel 97); it adds a layering of the respectable murder mystery to the more objectionable sexual romp.

Other changes in the scene are readily noticeable. Reinhold Niebuhr cited its immoderate length in the film (69), but in the novel it is even more drawn out—the speeches are longer, and the actions, both internal and external, are rendered with microscopic particularity. Humbert discloses, in fact, that the "whole sad business had taken more than an hour" (*Lolita* 306). Kubrick condenses the segment mightily, and one instance of his technique may serve to represent a multitude of others. In the book, an increasingly desperate Quilty attempts to dissuade Humbert from using his gun by delivering a speech—"Now look here, Mac," it begins—that wends its way for more than a page and contains roughly 500 words (303–4). The playwright argues that they are both men of the world, insists he took Lolita to a happier home, offers the house as a bribe, reminds Humbert of possible legal consequences, hints that he might give Humbert money, and mentions a collection of erotica upstairs. Kubrick cuts this windy declamation to: "Now look here, Mac. You're drunk and I'm a sick man. This pistol-packing farce is becoming sort of a nuisance."

The novel's version of Humbert's revenge is not only rangier but more gruesome. As Quilty hysterically plays piano, Humbert shoots him "somewhere in the side, and he [rises] from his chair higher and higher, … head thrown back in a howl …" (*Lolita* 304). Quilty then scurries through a hall and starts up a flight of stairs, whereupon Humbert fires "three or four times in quick succession, wounding him at every blaze" (305). Reloading, Humbert discovers that his hands are black and bloody—he has touched something "anointed with … thick gore" (305). His next shot tears off one of his victim's ears (306). Coughing and spitting, Quilty falls into bed, allowing Humbert to blast him at "very close range"; a "big pink bubble" forms on the dying man's lips, grows to the size of a toy balloon, and disappears (306). This last horrific image is almost identical to one that occurs in the film *Deliverance,* but Kubrick, some 10 years before, would skirt it completely in his sanitized *Lolita*.

Lolita Discovered

The story proper begins with a title informing us that we have been transported four years into the past. Sprightly music plays, generic travel scenes are shown, and the cultured voice of Humbert Humbert provides a synopsis of his situation at that juncture. A European translator of French poetry, he has just arrived in the United States. He hopes to spend a peaceful summer in Ramsdale,

New Hampshire, before moving on in the fall to a lectureship at Beardsley College, Ohio.

We register, first, the use of a voice-over, which may be taken both as a continuation and a change. Apart from the foreword, supposedly penned by the pompous John Ray, Jr., Humbert's voice is everywhere throughout the fictional text; it *is* the text. As such, we are neither surprised nor disturbed when the same voice intrudes itself in the film. (It recurs at polite intervals, now philosophizing about nymphets as Humbert writes in his journal, now giving a helpful summary that prods the fabula to its next phase.) But if the novel's narrator is garrulous to a fault, this new voice is subdued, terse, and measured. Though it operates in concert with the other elements of the text to privilege Humbert's point of view, the story no longer channels through him. The narration has been nudged some distance, therefore, from a strict, first-person orientation toward the film equivalent of a third-person limited approach (Martin 133–35). As a result, our perception of what happens becomes slightly more detached and balanced.

Of larger significance is the enormous volume of material that has been lopped from the original's lead-in. One is startled to find that, except for a few vague and scattered remnants, the film eliminates virtually all of the novel's foreword and first nine chapters. (Corresponding nicely with the film, Chapter 10 begins: "Upon signing out [of a sanitarium], I cast around for some place in the New England countryside or sleepy small town … where I could spend a studious summer …" [*Lolita* 37].) Excluded from the film are episodes, characters, and pieces of information that furnish the novel with some of its depth and resonance. In the book, we learn that Humbert's mother died from being hit by lightning when he was three, and that he was raised by his carefree father and his rigid Aunt Sybil (12). We learn that Lolita had a precursor, a girl named Annabel Leigh, with whom Humbert had a frustrating, adolescent interlude, and who, like his mother, died suddenly (13–15). We learn of his deep-seated fixation on nymphets, of his misadventures with prostitutes, of his dreary marriage to, and comical separation from, Valeria (18–32). Perhaps most notably, we learn of Humbert's bouts of "insanity"—his word—which required his confinement on three occasions (35–36).

The effect of the editing is twofold. First, it attenuates the story, reducing not only its length but its heft. What *Lolita* loses in substance, however, it regains in speed and agility, and now it comes at the audience in an undelayed rush. Second, the disposal of the background matter produces a new and more palatable Humbert, one more mysterious for his unstated history, and yet, so far as we can tell, more socially, morally, and psychologically conventional. From the outset, the Humbert of the novel has had a peculiar and ill-fated life. He is, to say the least, unwholesome; Nabokov himself pronounced him a "pervert" ("On a Book" 318). By contrast, Kubrick's Humbert arrives at the door of our consciousness fresh, unsullied, and without baggage. Though he may presently tumble into some predicament, his first condition asks viewers, including those who would censor, to withhold their judgment.

In the film, Humbert is given a tour, by Charlotte Haze, of his prospective residence. Smoking with a cigarette holder, murmuring bad French, and dropping double entendres—Hartung called her an "affected slob" (401)—she fails to impress Humbert. Culturally, she claims, she is a member of a "very advanced group," one that is "very progressive intellectually." She then speaks of her decidedly provincial club, demonstrates the bathroom's "old-fashioned, quaint plumbing," and shows off a collection of "reproductions" hanging in her bedroom. She mentions her deceased husband, whose ashes she keeps in the bedroom, and notes that, because he was in the insurance business, he was able to leave her "well-provided for." Twice she thrusts her bosom against Humbert's arm, each time drawing a quizzical look. He is on the verge of bolting when she takes him to see the garden, where shapely Lolita lounges in a broad-brimmed hat, shades, and a bikini. Sun in his face, a literal flash of illumination, Humbert agrees instantly to move in, giving as his reason Charlotte's offer of "cherry pies."

The scene follows Chapter 10 of Part One rather closely. Deviations occur, but they are predominantly minor. Nabokov's Charlotte is less brassy than Kubrick's (or Shelley Winters'); she and Humbert make no visit to her bedroom; and the reference to the "late Mr. Haze" is minted for the film. All these adjustments undercut the image, not sterling to begin, of Charlotte. By rendering her less sympathetic, more vulgar, and by doing the reverse with Humbert, the film encourages us to side with him; his squeamishness becomes ours, too. The normalizing of Humbert continues with the one major change the scene presents: the physical appearance of Lolita. The fictional nymphet, at age 12, stands four feet ten, has brown hair, and measures a sylphid 27–23–29 (*Lolita* 11; 50; 109). The gulf between that child and the blond siren of the film is immense. Although actress Sue Lyon was 14 when the film was shot, reviewers put her apparent age at 17 or 18 (Hartung 401; "Humbert Humdrum" 94; MacDonald 45). Again, the effect is to suggest that Humbert's actions, if not defensible, are now quite understandable. A story originally told from the edge of a moral abyss is fast moving toward safer ground.

A series of brief scenes follows as Humbert settles into life in Ramsdale. Seated to his right in a theater, Lolita grasps his knee during a horror film, and he pats her hand as if to comfort her; she then throws her other hand on top of his. Both seem abashed when these shenanigans are discovered by Charlotte, who is seated to his left. Next, Humbert and Charlotte play a chess game laden with symbolism. "You're going to take my queen?" she wonders. "That is my intention," he replies, and, receiving a nuzzling good-night kiss from Lolita, he proceeds to capture the queen. Now, clad in a bathrobe, Humbert sits mesmerized outside as Lolita practices with her hula hoop. Charlotte steps out, snaps his picture, and commends him for becoming so relaxed—a gross misinterpretation of Humbert's state at that moment.

Each of these scenes is rooted in the novel, but, in every case, Kubrick carefully alters the prototype. The first episode, the groping at the theater, has its fictional counterpart in a trip taken by the three principals to the store. As Charlotte drives, Lolita slips her hand unseen into Humbert's, and he holds and "stroke[s] and squeeze[s] that little hot paw" (*Lolita* 53); it is a blunt development that the film tames into ambiguity and even comedy. Of course the original Humbert does play chess, but the games appear later in the narrative, when he and Lolita have relocated to Beardsley. His opponent is not Charlotte—she is long dead—but Gaston Godin, a "freakish" and effeminate character whose absence from the film

Chapter 2. Lolita

Although Humbert's chess-playing partner of the novel is omitted from the film, the game itself, with its symbolic import, is retained.

streamlines it and keeps it nearer the center of American tastes (183). Finally, Nabokov's Lolita does not wriggle in a hula hoop; she sits next to Humbert, picks up pebbles between her sneakered feet, and flips them at a sliver of milk-bottle glass, a movement that sends Humbert nearly into ecstasy (43). Few except him would find this innocent activity stimulating, hence the business with the hula hoop, which, as Raymond Durgnat allowed, is a blatantly "erotic [but not lewd] idea" (35).

The film takes us next to a formal dance that seems to have attracted a healthy percentage of Ramsdale's population. Humbert and Charlotte are in attendance, as are Lolita and her friend Kenny, John and Jean Farlow and their daughter Mona, and Clare Quilty and his somber, silent female companion whom readers of the book know as Vivian Darkbloom. Humbert appears dismayed that Lolita is with a boy, and that the boy is planning to ask her to go steady. John and Jean are a pushy, abrasive couple preoccupied with sex; he dances with Charlotte while Jean flirts with Humbert. Momentarily separated from Humbert, who has crept away, Charlotte accosts the local celebrity Clare Quilty, presently in mid-dance with his friend. Charlotte finishes the dance with him and reminds him in a whisper of something he once did with her or to her. As at the start of the film, Quilty's memory is patchy, though he does recall Lolita. Humbert grimaces when he learns that Lolita will spend the night at John and Jean's—the news means Humbert and Charlotte will be alone together in her house.

No such dance is seen in the novel—we get a passing allusion to one later in the narrative (*Lolita* 193)—but its presence in the film is instrumental. The ongoing theme of a naughty and pervasive sexuality is underlined; Charlotte's aggressiveness continues apace, and is easily matched by that of John and Jean. Set against these characters, Humbert ironically (but deliberately) seems a paragon of dignity and restraint—he declines even to dance. Structurally, a good deal of compression is evidenced. In the novel, Charlotte drags Humbert on a loosely analogous picnic at Hourglass Lake with Lolita and Mary Rose Hamilton (58). Much later, we get a glimpse of a girl named Mona—but she is not the Farlows' daughter and does not live in Ramsdale (192–93). In fact, we do not meet John and Jean until after Humbert and Charlotte are married (80–81). The easygoing pace of the novel is being hurried along. Interestingly, the role of one character, Clare Quilty, is beginning here to expand. He, and not Humbert, represents evil in the film, and must be given a size equal to his duty.

After the dance, Humbert's fears are realized as Charlotte, at home, tries relentlessly to seduce him. Changed into a low-cut, tiger-print dress, she pours pink champagne, turns on cha-cha music, and proposes to teach Humbert "some of the new steps." Soon she has him awkwardly dancing. His interest in Charlotte is nil, and he resists her overtures as sincerely as his "Old World" manners will permit. The standoff ends when Lolita returns home unexpectedly, to his pleasure and to Charlotte's annoyance. In due course Charlotte compels her daughter to go upstairs, but only after the two have exchanged words. With Lolita gone, Charlotte rants about her, charging that the girl has become "impossible." Humbert dryly thanks his landlady for a "charming evening" and goes, by himself, to bed.

The dance scene, invented for the film, enables Kubrick to compress the narrative and quicken its pace.

Despite its growth out of the interpolated dance scene, the foregoing sequence adheres to the spirit, and sometimes the letter, of the novel. Kubrick's few changes work to the detriment of Charlotte, magnifying her undesirable qualities. Nabokov's Charlotte sits with Humbert on the piazza and, while Lolita squirms between them, discusses a film she has seen (*Lolita* 47). As in the adaptation, Charlotte becomes impatient and orders Lolita to bed. "I think you stink," comes the reply, and "This is a free country" (48), language that Kubrick retains. After Lolita departs, Charlotte grumbles about her, and Humbert retires—only to have Charlotte ask through his door if he is done with a certain *Glance and Gulp* magazine he has borrowed (49). But aside from this forwardness at the door, the Charlotte of the film is more brazen than the original, practically launching herself at Humbert. She is also more noxious, rambling angrily in Winters' diva voice; the fictional Charlotte condemns her daughter in nothing but indirect quotations, a device that distances the reader from her fury. Again, the film craftily maneuvers us away from Charlotte and toward Humbert; it asks us to take his side, to view him with sympathy.

Morning finds Humbert in his room, scribbling in his journal. His obsession with Lolita, though hitherto implied, is now articulated via voice-over: "What drives me insane," he confesses, "is the twofold nature of this nymphet, of every nymphet perhaps: this mixture in my Lolita of tender, dreamy childishness, and a kind of eerie vulgarity." He locks the journal away when Lolita brings him breakfast. Sidestepping her questions, he reads her a fragment of Poe's "Ulalume," a poem she judges "corny." She is about to confide something about her friend Mona, but then reconsiders, fearing he might "blab." Humbert promises to respect her secrets, and she playfully offers him a reward: "one little bite" of a fried egg that she dangles over his mouth. Convulsively, he takes an enormous bite. She leaves when her mother calls her away.

This short scene smoothly accomplishes several ends. First, Kubrick appropriately pays homage to the "divine Edgar," whose influence permeates the novel. (In a work bristling with literary allusions, Poe is invoked more than anyone, ahead of Mérimée, Shakespeare, and Joyce [Appel 331].) One recalls, incidentally, that "Ulalume" sees "Hope" and "Beauty" transformed into tragedy and despair (Poe line 65), a theme not vastly dissimilar from *Lolita*'s. More significantly, Kubrick mutes Humbert's ravings about nymphets, who, he explains in the novel, are "not human, but ... demoniac," and who are detectable only by a "madman, a creature of infinite melancholy, with a bubble of hot poison in [his] loins" (*Lolita* 18–19). In fact, the original screenplay incorporated more of this spiel, but was rewritten due to concerns over censorship (Walker, *Sex in the Movies* 173). In this vein, the fictional Humbert's lust for Lolita is expressed directly and unmistakably; as described in a near-pornographic passage, he takes her legs across his "live lap"—he is wearing a robe; she, pajamas—fondles her, and, as she climbs more fully onto him, he brings himself secretly to an orgasm (*Lolita* 60–63). One appreciates Kubrick's ingenuity in substituting a ravenous bite from a fried egg for an act of frottage: the desired message is conveyed, but lightly.

That evening, Charlotte informs Humbert that she is sending Lolita off to camp, 200 miles away, with Mona. He is pained at the news, but explains his discomfort as a toothache. Next morning, he is awakened by the sounds, from outside his open window, of the Haze station wagon's being readied for the trip. Spying him, Lolita scampers back upstairs to give him a farewell kiss, and leaves him that he might stagger forlorn into her room. Abruptly the maid, Louise, hands him a note from Charlotte that he reads aloud. The landlady indicates that she loves Humbert, and has from the start. She asks him to move out at once; if he does not, it can only mean that he wants to link his life with hers forever, and is willing to be a father to Lolita. The missive reduces him to a howl of helpless laughter, but it also presents him with a fateful decision. From the wall, a picture of Quilty stares down at him, and at us.

These events are patterned after those of Chapters 14 through 16, Part One. The film deviates from the novel in only a few instances, to slight but predictable effect. Inspiration for the novel's camping trip comes not from the childless Farlows, but from a Mrs. Chatfield, who is sending her daughter Phyllis away (*Lolita* 65). Clearly the film retreats from a profusion of names, keeping before us known characters who inhabit a relatively simple and lean plot. Whereas in the novel Humbert is told on Sunday that Lolita will be taken from him on Thursday (65), the film has her leaving the very next morning; the time line has been shortened. Similarly, Charlotte's plaintive note to Humbert is slashed for the film by perhaps two-thirds—more than that, if we accept the narrator's aside that the "real" note was "at least twice longer" than his years-later reconstruction of it (70). The original Humbert's reaction to the note, by the way, is "one of repulsion and retreat," soon hardening into cold calculation (71); it is much less appealing than the film's fit of laughter.

Following a prolonged blackout, we are given to understand that Humbert and Charlotte have recently married. But beneath the surface, little has changed. Humbert, writing in his journal (and speaking to us through voice-over), dismisses the wedding as a "quiet affair" and refers to a "conspiratorial dagger" that he is sharpening, presumably, for his wife. As he jots down his thoughts in the bathroom, Charlotte, barred by a locked door, pesters him about his premarital love life. He finally emerges and they go to the bedroom where she shows him her late husband's handgun. While they cuddle in bed, she reveals her plan to send Lolita straight from camp to a boarding school, and then on to college. This scenario prompts Humbert to pursue a dark "train of thought," during which pursuit he first stares at a photograph of Lolita, then eyes the gun, which is resting on a stand next to the bed. Lolita calls from camp and, speaking to Charlotte, wants to thank Humbert for the candy he has sent her. Charlotte scolds her husband for not consulting her about the candy, causing him to bridle at being taken for a "lap dog." Charlotte flounces away, and Humbert now considers using the gun to kill her; he could claim that her death resulted from an accident. Surprising himself, he finds he is unable to carry out his intention. Even more surprising to him is Charlotte's invasion of his journal, whose cramped entries she proves able to decipher. Incensed, she calls him a "monster," promises to leave him, and then apostrophizes to her first husband, praising him as the "soul of integrity." We abandon her to rejoin Humbert, who mixes her a martini and insists, hollering from the kitchen, that his journal represents notes for a novel. The phone rings, and someone advises him, incredibly, that his wife is dead, struck by a car. Humbert steps outside into the rain and learns that the astonishing report is accurate.

This section is a model of condensation and artful distortion. The novel tells us, in detail, what Humbert does after reading Charlotte's note—he purchases food, liquor, and vitamins; drinks gin and pineapple juice; and mows the lawn (*Lolita* 74–75). For the sake of speed and focus, the film omits all these tidbits. The novel affords us an overview of the doomed marriage and its banalities: how Charlotte excuses herself after burping, how her looks seem to improve, how she habitually watches with "tenderness" as Humbert consumes his morning ham and eggs (77; 78; 79). The film shrinks this overview to simply a view, and one that covers minutes, not weeks. In the novel, Humbert fantasizes about drowning his wife at the lake (86–89); the episode is dropped from the film, though many of its particulars, including snippets of the language, are grafted onto the near murder by gun in the film. If, in the novel, she poses "businesslike" questions about the table in which Humbert secures his journal (94), she gives it no more than a glance in the film. To be sure, his quest for a sleeping potion with which he might violate Lolita is excised completely from the film (96); the excision saves time and, as much, whatever regard we may have for the protagonist. Like Ben Jonson, Kubrick challenges us to see beauties in small proportions.

But the original materials are not only trimmed and tightened; they are manipulated in interesting ways. Kubrick has written of his fondness for the so-called objective correlative (306). The term was introduced by T. S. Eliot, who believed that the

> only way of expressing emotion in the form of art is by finding an "objective correlative"; in other words, a set of objects, a situation, a chain of events which shall be the formula of that *particular* emotion; such that when the external facts, which must terminate in sensory experience, are given, the emotion is immediately evoked ["Hamlet" 100].

We encounter a superb example of this principle in action as Humbert tosses in bed with Charlotte. To one side, he is faced with a photograph of Lolita; to the other, a gun—the dichotomy does not exist in the novel. When he gazes at either of these objects, we receive a distinct, if primitive, sense of what he is thinking and feeling; no subtitle could better suggest his turmoil.

One is also struck by the moving soliloquy Charlotte delivers in her last appearance. Alone in the bedroom, her life in tatters, she addresses her late husband—his picture, his ashes—in heartfelt tones. She admits her disloyalty to his memory, explaining that seven years a widow is a long span. Then she turns spitefully on him: "Why did you go and die on me?" she wails. "If you hadn't died, all this wouldn't've happened." Her mood shifting again, she weeps and asks his forgiveness, and vows that the next man in her life will be someone that Mr. Haze will be "very proud of." The incident does not exist in the book, and its effect here is to humanize Charlotte, who has been something of a caricature to this stage. The film reminds us that her life counts, as much as Humbert's and Lolita's, and that her faults (and Humbert's) may have unfunny consequences. Such didacticism, though foreign to Nabokov, is typical of Hollywood. One also speculates that her *cri de coeur* is a star turn, a chance for Shelley Winters to exhibit her virtuosic skills as an actress in her final stint before the camera.

Lolita Acquired

Though the film, like the novel, has its solemn moments, it is loath to stay deeply serious for long. In the aftermath of Charlotte's death, Humbert lies immersed in his bathtub, serenely sipping from a glass of whiskey. John and Jean Farlow come wandering through the house searching for him, and Humbert, quietly but definitely inebriated, invites them into the bathroom. Consoling him, or attempting to, they notice the gun, which he has placed near the sink, and wrongly conclude that he is thinking of suicide. They then console him further, noting that Charlotte had only one kidney, and probably would have died soon, anyway. Now another visitor, Frederick Beale, Sr., the father of the man whose car killed Charlotte, makes his way into the crowded bathroom. Smiling vacuously, Beale asserts that the accident was technically the pedestrian's fault, not the driver's, and Humbert graciously agrees. When Beale offers to pay the funeral expenses, Humbert pleasantly agrees once more.

Drawn from Chapters 23 and 24 of Part One, this amusing sequence is much less farcical in the novel. There, Humbert seems genuinely rattled, not so much by Charlotte's demise, but by the pitfalls still lurking between him and Lolita: the Farlows might find him out, or Lolita herself might betray "some foolish distrust of [him], a sudden repugnance, ... and gone would be the magic prize at the very instant of triumph" (*Lolita* 103–4). In fact, the Farlows' concern for both him and his stepdaughter is marked (101–3), and Humbert, yielding to some belated torment, ultimately breaks down in tears (105). But the film plays the scene for irreverent humor, showcasing Humbert in his bathtub—no such vision occurs in the book—and overlaying ditsy theme music to ensure our proper interpretation. The only example of the novel's trumping the film's absurdity is seen in the visit of Beale (Jr., and not Sr.), who unrolls a large diagram, replete with arrows and dotted lines, depicting the accident

(104). The prop goes unused by Kubrick, an omission that allows for a quicker, less cluttered exchange. Confounding the poignancy of Charlotte's last words, the bathtub scene stresses the film's resolve to be lighter and less threatening than its source.

Humbert, availing himself of Charlotte's station wagon, drives to Camp Climax for Girls, where Lolita awaits him. He chats uneasily with Charlie, a smug boy who works at the camp, and then drives away with Lolita, who is still ignorant of her mother's death. He tells her that Charlotte is sick, and has been taken to a hospital near Lepingsville; his announced plan calls for them to spend the night in a hotel in Briceland, and to press on toward Lepingsville in the morning. After a sustained pause, Humbert declares that he has missed Lolita terribly. She answers saucily that she has been "revoltingly unfaithful" to him, and chides him for not having kissed her yet.

This section is almost purely a distillation of the novel's corresponding pages. What happens in the film happens also in the book, but much of what happens in the book is gone from the film. En route to the camp, the fictional Humbert calls its mistress from Parkington, where he later buys "beautiful things" for Lolita and spends a restless night (*Lolita* 108–11). Next morning, he must overcome a dead battery (112). Having collected Lolita, he chats with her at some length—she expresses revulsion at cows, reproves Humbert for driving too fast, and describes some of her activities at camp (114–16). The deletion of this texture obviously hastens the narrative, but manages to preserve its essential meaning. Then too, by erasing all but one of Lolita's hints that she has misbehaved sexually, the film is able to retain its moderately wholesome veneer.

We are given an establishing shot of the hotel, then an interior shot of the lobby where Quilty and his dark lady, vacationing together, approach Mr. Swine, the desk clerk. Quilty engages Swine in small talk ripe with sexual innuendo. When Humbert and Lolita enter, Quilty retreats to the end of the long desk; he remains visible in the background, spying on the newcomers. With some difficulty—the hotel is burdened by a police convention—Humbert arranges for a room. (The room has just one bed, and cots are scarce.) He and Lolita go to the room, and she supposes that if her mother were to learn of this setup, Charlotte would divorce him and strangle her. Yawning in bed, Lolita suggests that he should try again to locate a cot.

As before, one recognizes an overall conformity to the novel. It generally predicts Humbert's and Lolita's movements, and many of their comments: he discusses with Swine the availability of a cot, and she mentions the possibility of divorce and strangulation (*Lolita* 120–21). But one also perceives some key differences between the texts that betoken their unique personalities. The novel contains no reference to a police convention, though Humbert does sign the register in the "slow clear hand of crime" (120)—so here a subjective impression has become a palpable circumstance, one that warns Humbert, and us, that he is doing something shameful. In the novel, Lolita identifies what that something is. As Humbert sputters vaguely, trying to rationalize why they happen to be together in the same room, she cuts him off with: "The word is incest" (121). The same word, and others equally unkind, are applicable in the film, but they remain unspoken, their harshness safely suppressed. The fictional Humbert softens Lolita's defenses with his bribe (he calls it his "surprise") of new clothing (122), and then tricks her into taking what he believes is a powerful sleeping agent by telling her it is "Vitamin X. Makes one strong as an ox or an ax" (124). Keeping the film Humbert removed from such tawdriness does not exalt him, but it does prevent him from sliding even farther into moral muck. Turning away from the central couple, we notice that Quilty, who is no more than a phantom throughout most of the novel—"the lone diner in the loud checks" (123)—continues to take on a larger role; his mundane evil, as contradistinguished from Humbert's romantic evil, is being brought to substantial life. As with Winters, one suspects that Peter Sellers' stardom demands this wider presence—but so perhaps does the film medium, which often personifies evil (Madsen 263; "Mass Appeals" 336).

Drink in hand, Humbert meanders through the lobby, and then goes outside to sit on the dimly lit veranda. He is soon joined by Quilty, who, with his back to him, begins a strange, probing, circular conversation. Pretending to be a police officer, Quilty repeatedly compliments Humbert on how "normal" and unsuspicious he seems—implying that Humbert is actually quite abnormal and highly suspicious. He inquires about Humbert's wife and "daughter" (as Humbert has identified Lolita); he also asks to see Humbert and Lolita's room, and to join them for breakfast. Disentangling himself from the cross-examination, Humbert returns to the room, where a porter is bent on bringing in, and setting up, a cot. Since Humbert hopes not to awaken Lolita, and since the cot is almost willfully recalcitrant, their strained, silent attempts to unfold the thing make for slapstick humor. After the porter leaves, Humbert tries to slip into bed with Lolita. She stirs from her sleep just long enough to discourage him, and he repairs to the cot.

As in the film, the fictional Humbert encounters Quilty on a dark, "pillared porch" (*Lolita* 128), but originally their meeting is shorter and more enigmatic. In the film, we have some idea of who Quilty is and what he is about, but at the same point in the novel, he is barely a character; he exists more as a set of veiled allusions, a fleeting image, a voice in the night. The fictional Quilty speaks just seven times in this passage, and then in crisp, pithy statements that contrast vividly with the film's logorrhea:

"Who's the lassie?"
"My daughter."
"You lie—she's not."
"I beg your pardon?"
"I said: July was hot" [129].

In placing the texts side by side, it becomes clear that the film Quilty is more commanding of narrative space, and is sketched more boldly. It is also arguable that "policeman" Quilty's words, hammering as they do on suspicion and normality, are more manifestly designed to play on Humbert's conscience, and on ours. In this respect, the film seems to worry more about segregating traditional right and wrong than does the novel.

The foolery with the cot is wholly invented for the film; Humbert is told, in the novel, that a cot "would be installed tomorrow if [they] decided to stay on" (*Lolita* 128). Since the prop does not really figure in the book beyond being mentioned, one is led to reflect on its function in the film. Certainly the men's loony skirmish with it provides comic relief: relief from the witty but disturbing dialog with Quilty, and from the anxiety generated by what Humbert calls "*le grand moment*" (125): what *will* this man do when he gets his chance with the girl? It also fits with, and helps to determine, the film's relatively light approach—nothing truly sinister is happening here, the message seems to be; what we are witnessing is just harmless sport. More deeply, if Freud was right in his belief that jokes provide a view to the unconscious, one might conclude that the film has grown nervous about its own content: that it is unwilling or unable to deal seriously with a serious topic. Even as Humbert displays a facial tic in moments of tension, so might the cot business be construed as the film's jitteriness about itself.

Morning breaks through the window, and Lolita climbs out of bed wearing a nightgown and an impish smile. She goes to the head of Humbert's collapsed cot, on which he lies sleeping. "Wake up, Humbert!" she says excitedly. "The hotel's on fire!" He grumbles at this juvenile humor, but she lingers affectionately over him, checking his watch, comparing her tan to his, stroking the stubble on his cheeks. "Well," she murmurs after a while, "what should we do now?" He recommends she ring down and order breakfast. But she has a different desire, which she communicates to him by whispering in his ear. Truncated, the scene goes to black.

This short sequence marks a cusp in the narrative. Humbert, who hopes to seduce Lolita, is instead seduced by her. Kubrick, of course, manages this development with an adroitness so seamless as to have disappointed some critics. "The movie gives only the most fugitive, embarrassed version of the [original] scene," Dwight MacDonald wrote (46). "The sex," Andrew Sarris ventured, "is so discreetly handled that an unsophisticated spectator may be completely mystified" (11). Yet a close examination of the novel reveals that Nabokov's methods and Kubrick's are not radically different— not, at least, so far as Kubrick chooses to extend the scene. In the novel, Humbert and Lolita, absent the cot, begin the morning in bed together. He caresses her hair, and they kiss (*Lolita* 135). She then whispers something in his ear, and the sex play begins—but the reader is not privy to it. Reluctant to "bore [his] learned readers with a detailed account of Lolita's presumption" (135), Humbert keeps his account both general and economical. We learn—later— that they have "strenuous intercourse" three times that morning

(142), but the comment goes unembroidered. What Kubrick omits—and what Nabokov presents (but still distantly)—is Lolita's synopsis of her prior sexual experience (138–39). By ending the scene when he does, Kubrick achieves compression and maintains cleanliness; yet he excludes only a little that Nabokov has not already withheld.

Humbert and Lolita resume their expedition toward Lepingsville, and we join them inside the car. Munching potato chips and sipping a soft drink, she carries the bulk of the conversation. She wishes she could kiss the Blarney stone, teases him about perhaps spilling to Charlotte some unspecified secret the two share, mourns for a "squashed" cat along the road, yearns for french fries and a malt, and hopes to see a film in the evening—but not a foreign one. She requests that they stop at a service station so she can call her mother at the hospital. Humbert resists. When she presses to know why he does not want her to call her mother, he hesitates, then answers: "Because your mother is dead."

Skipping ahead to that evening, the narrative locates the couple in a tenebrous motel room. She lies sobbing in one bed while he lies in another, silently agonizing. At last, still crying, she falls into his bed, and he tries to comfort her. "Nothing will ever be all right," she says, and adds: "Everything is changed.... Everything was so, oh I don't know, normal." He proposes that they find a new home in Beardsley, where he will lecture. The possessions she misses from Ramsdale will be sent for or replaced. She admits her fear of being banished to a place for "juvenile delinquents," and he promises, three times, never to allow that fate to befall her.

Set against the original text, the foregoing pair of scenes emerges as a clever combination of additions, cuts, and modulations. Most of the dialog spoken in the car is new, and quickly reaffirms the cultural chasm between the characters. Humbert is not only decades older than Lolita, but, for all his faults, genuinely cosmopolitan: a traveled scholar. Lolita, on the other hand, lives in a world in which complex emotion means feeling sympathy for a dead cat; in which *haute cuisine* points to french fries; in which artistic discrimination consists in rejecting the same foreign films that he admires. This crucial disjuncture between the lovers is hardly ignored by Nabokov, but he explores it over pages and chapters; Kubrick crystallizes it in a single conversation. At the same time, some elements of the original have been conspicuously dropped. The novel's Lolita seems to have been injured during sex (*Lolita* 142), and teases Humbert more crassly than her film counterpart: "You revolting creature," she buffets him. "I was a daisy-fresh girl, and look what you've done to me. I ought to call the police and tell them you raped me. Oh, you dirty, dirty old man" (143). Here, as elsewhere, Kubrick carefully controls his film's outspokenness. He also softens and romanticizes the bond that holds the couple together. If, in the film, Humbert sweetly promises never to send Lolita off to a reformatory, he threatens her, in the novel, with that very outcome: "You [will] become a ward of the Department of Public Welfare.... A nice grim matron ... will take away your lipstick and fancy clothes" (153). The fictional Humbert is, as Lolita contends, a "brute" (142), but Kubrick invites us to accept the film version as something of a "sensitive and intelligent man whose emotional needs and compulsions overpower, let us say, his moral sense" (Alpert 40).

Beardsley

Humbert's voice-over adjures us to forget Ramsdale, since, by now, six months have passed, and he and Lolita are living in Beardsley. Revisiting the opening tableau, a pensive Humbert paints Lolita's toenails. He asks her why she was so late in coming home from school yesterday, and she replies that she and her friend Michelle stayed to watch football practice. But Humbert says he spotted her in the Frigid Queen, sitting with boys; he does not want her to date. She admits she was in the place, but denies she was dating as such. Expanding his inquiry, he wants to know why she was late last Saturday, and why Michelle has been giving him "searching looks"—has Lolita confessed the true nature of her relationship with Humbert? She denies any wrongdoing, and complains that he never allows her to have fun; he defends himself as a solicitous protector and companion. With shrewd timing, she asks his permission to perform in the school play. Humbert, who suspects that the play would be a means for her to consort with "nasty-minded" boys, refuses, precipitating a quarrel.

One notices immediately that the film purges a long and significant section of the fictional tale: Humbert's (or Nabokov's) beautifully written record of the couple's "extensive travels all over the States" (*Lolita* 147). Their journey takes a full year, from August 1947 to August 1948 (156), and consumes some 30 pages of the novel. A striking evocation of America, touching on many of its strengths and many of its foibles, the pertinent passage also dwells on the discord arising between the travelers: the "shared secrecy and shared guilt" Humbert seeks to establish (153), the bitter "rows" they endure (160), and her "sobs in the night—every night, every night—the moment [he feigns] sleep" (178). By omitting the travelog, which does little to propel the fabula forward—Kristin Thompson would term it a "free motif" (38)—and by transferring some of its friction to the toe-painting scene, Kubrick not only conserves time but captures, in diluted form, some of the original's jagged emotion.

The scene itself pulls together tightly a number of items that are spaced over several chapters in the novel. While still on the road, Humbert catalogs all the "sunny nothings" he bestows on Lolita that supposedly prove he is fun to be with (*Lolita* 165); in the film, he reels off a similar, if abbreviated, list. In the novel, it is Humbert who visits a "milk bar" called the Frigid Queen (168); though the incident is altered for the film, the name of the restaurant, with its sly connotation, is happily preserved. The fictional Humbert, like the film Humbert, is dedicated to keeping Lolita from socializing with boys:

> Absolutely forbidden were dates, single, double or triple…. I was quite positive that as long as my regime lasted she would never, never be permitted to go with a youngster in rut to a movie, or neck in a car, or go to boy-girl parties at the houses of schoolmates, or indulge out of my earshot in boy-girl telephone conversations [188].

Despite his restrictions, he sights her, as he does in the film, with occasional faceless "chappies" (189). Lolita's desire to act in a play is likewise vouched in the novel, but relatively later in the Beardsley segment. By converging all these scattered references into one scene, the film retains many of the book's flavorful nuggets, but delivers them at an accelerated pace. (Two lurid details that do not survive adaptation are Lolita's practice of charging Humbert a fee for sex, and his of stealing the money back [186]; Kubrick's subject is forbidden love, not forbidden commerce.)

Humbert drives home one evening to discover a stranger sitting in his darkened living room, patiently awaiting him. The man politely introduces himself as Dr. Zempf, the Beardsley High School psychologist; we recognize him as Quilty. Speaking with an exaggerated German accent, Quilty inquires if anyone has instructed Lolita in the "facts of life"; the onset of maturity, he states, is giving her trouble at school. She is defiant and rude, sighs and giggles excessively, and shows poor concentration. It would seem that she is suffering from a repressed libido, and Quilty suggests that Dr. Cutler, a psychologist, and his three-member board be brought into Humbert's home to investigate the source of Lolita's problem. Visibly disturbed, Humbert refuses the suggestion out of hand. As an alternative, Quilty proposes that Lolita be allowed wider participation in the school's extracurricular projects. Specifically, she should be permitted to act in the school play, and to date and dance as she likes. Humbert is acquiescent.

His unexpected interview with Quilty-as-Zempf has its genesis in Chapter 11, Part Two of the novel. There, Humbert is called in to school to be grilled by Headmistress Pratt, a huge, frowsy woman who is puzzled over "Dolly's" poor scholarship and vaguely maladjusted behavior (*Lolita* 195). In all, the fictional and film conversations proceed along similar lines, and arrive at the same conclusion: that Humbert should rescind his order forbidding Lolita's participation in the dramatic group. But material differences in what gets said, and in how the scenes are handled, assert themselves. The original exchange is longer—Pratt is even more voluble than Sellers' Quilty—and franker; she pictures Lolita as "shuttling between the anal and genital zones of development" (196). The omissions that obtain here do not surprise. Though Pratt mentions a Dr. Cutler (199), nothing is said about his entering Humbert's household with three of his staff in tow; this addition of the film's puts a surplus of pressure on Humbert, and makes his nemesis seem all the more devilish. Most obviously, Pratt's words, those that remain, are assigned to the nefarious Quilty. Again, his part in the narrative is augmented, and, since he is pitted against Humbert, we appreciate that we cannot root for one without rooting against the other. The film's opening, which exposes Quilty's callousness and foretells his defeat, guides us in our rooting: Humbert is being structurally positioned as the "hero." Beyond these internal considerations, the scene provides Sellers a chance to exhibit his much-touted gift for mimicry (Alpert 40; "Humbert Humdrum" 94; Kauffmann, "Humbug" 29; Sarris 11).

We cut now to the school play, where Quilty lurks in the wings, and Lolita is made up, appropriately, as a nymph. A player's voice proclaims that the "bewitcher is bewitched," and Lolita emerges onstage to escort a goatish man to the "dark kingdom." When the performance ends, a pleased-looking Humbert is approached by Miss Starch, Lolita's flirtatious piano teacher. She dismays him with her casual revelation that, for the past four weeks, Lolita has not been attending her piano lessons. Angered at Lolita's duplicity, he seizes her, and, over her protests, forcibly takes her home.

Differences between the two incarnations of this sequence are clear-cut and instructive. First, the film tightens, or seems to tighten, the chronology of events. In the novel, Humbert's discussion with Pratt occurs sometime in December (*Lolita* 195), and rehearsals for the play are being held as late as May of the following year (204). But aside from Miss Starch's comment about the missed piano lessons, the film gives no clue that much time has elapsed, if indeed it has. Moreover, in terms of screen-time, the performance of the play trails Humbert's meeting with Zempf-Quilty by mere seconds; the viewer is fairly catapulted into the future. In concert with this tactic, the film dispenses with some details that bring richness to the novel: Humbert's opinion of theater (he detests it [202]); the name of the play—*The Enchanted Hunters* (202)—which corresponds to the name of the hotel wherein he first possesses Lolita, and which has thematic overtones; friend Mona's corroboration of Lolita's lie (205). We also note that the

Barely noticeable in the source, the fiendish Quilty—seen here as "Dr. Zempf"—becomes highly visible in the film.

piano teacher, "Miss Emperor" in the novel (204), seems to have adopted an aggressive new personality for the screen. By making her sexually predatory—"Do you play?" she asks Humbert—the film continues to frame Humbert as a model of restraint in a world peopled by lechers. Perhaps most remarkably, the play never actually gets performed in the novel—not even in part. By showing us the closing moment of *The Enchanted Hunters,* the film declares its natural affinity for visuality, dramatic liveliness, and immediacy.

When Humbert and Lolita arrive home, a loud, ugly altercation ensues. He insists on knowing how she has been spending her secret hours. After first denying that she has missed any piano lessons, she claims she has used the time to attend extra rehearsals. Humbert dismisses this possibility as a "fatuous lie," and accuses her of dallying with a boy. She pronounces him "sick." Weakening, he now says he accepts her shaky explanation, and urges that they leave Beardsley, which he deems a "horrible place" and the real cause of their troubles. Lolita resists, quietly at the start, and then with piercing, hateful screams. A neighbor, Miss Lebone, knocks on the door and gingerly complains about the racket; this interruption allows Lolita to slip out into the night. Soon after, Humbert finds her in a phone booth. He pulls her out to learn that she has apparently undergone a change of heart: she wants to reconcile with Humbert, and to leave Beardsley with him.

The shape of this pivotal quarrel and its aftermath is predicted with broad accuracy by the novel. What transpires in the film, however, does diverge from the original in a few particulars. The fictional altercation is, for example, more raw in its content, and yet more distanced in its presentation. With regard to the first point, Nabokov's Lolita yells "unprintable things" (*Lolita* 207). She also defines Humbert as an attempted rapist and successful murderer, and vows to "sleep with the very first fellow who ask[s] her" (207). With regard to the second point, virtually all of her philippic is conveyed to the reader through diegesis and not mimesis—Humbert summarizes her explosive language, thereby keeping the reader at a discreet remove. These paired tendencies are reversed by the film, which checks her venom, but of course represents her statements, and her actions, directly. (The former eventuality is mandated by the latter.) In the novel, Miss Lebone's complaint is managed by telephone (208), whereas Kubrick has her step right into Humbert's company—again, the film recognizes the visual as much as, or more than, it does the verbal. Finally, the fictional Lolita makes her escape on a bicycle, a getaway vehicle perfectly suited to her youth (208). But the more womanly Lolita of the film flees on foot; to have plopped this character on a bike would have undercut her image of precocious maturity, and may have called attention to the perversity of her entire situation, a perversity that Kubrick has labored to downplay.

Flight from Beardsley

After a blackout, Humbert's voice-over describes how the station wagon has been reconditioned, and presently we see it cruising along the highway. Some days into this second voyage, Humbert notices that he and Lolita are being followed by a strange car that he interprets as a "designation of doom." His fear that something is amiss is heightened further when, through a washroom window at a gas station, he witnesses Lolita talking to a stranger in a parked car. Driving now at a breakneck speed, Humbert shares with Lolita his belief that someone is pursuing them, and that the pursuer may be "some kind of a cop"; she seems doubtful. As he quizzes her about the man she spoke to at the gas station, their car has a blowout, and they squeal to a stop along a deserted mountain road. The other car soon pulls up behind them, but at a certain distance, sending Humbert into a frenzy of paranoia. Compounding his misery, his arm has begun to hurt, and he has difficulty breathing. The rogue car suddenly turns around and drives off as Lolita begins to complain of flu symptoms.

This trip westward, from Ohio generally toward the Mexican border, makes for one of Kubrick's most extreme demonstrations of reduction. Beginning with Humbert and Lolita's departure and terminating with her fever, the sequence fills more than seven chapters of the novel, or roughly 30 pages (*Lolita* 210–41). From the book, Kubrick has taken fragments of language, and some—not many—rudiments of plot. Humbert's voice-over is excerpted from the first two paragraphs of Chapter 15, Part Two; his brooding over "designations of doom" is purely Nabokovian (219); and much of the dialog is drawn from the original. Concerning the plot, Kubrick fastens on these aspects of the fictional narrative: Lolita appears to be in contact with an outsider (220); Humbert understands he is being trailed by someone that he thinks is a "cop" (219–20); the station wagon suffers a flat tire in "mountain country" (230); and the pursuer pauses some 50 yards behind, then executes a U-turn, and drives away (230–31). Yet for all these correspondences between the texts, deletions to the original are voluminous. In the novel, the travelers make a side-trip to Kasbeam, some 30 miles from Lolita's hometown (214–15); they see a play (written by Clare Quilty and Vivian Darkbloom) in Wace (222–23); they pick up mail, forwarded to a post office box, from Beardsley (224–25); Lolita disappears for 28 minutes, then reappears (225–27); she plays tennis at a Colorado resort (232–34). All these excisions and more bring about compression; the gist of the story is maintained, though many of its niceties are abandoned. Two other eye-catching cuts uphold Humbert's improved image in the film. The fictional Humbert, convinced that Lolita has been with another man, rips off her clothes to sniff for the scent of her infidelity (217). Much later, he strikes her—a "tremendous backhand cut that [catches] her smack on her hot hard little cheekbone" (229). A panoramic excursion has been shrunk to little more than a series of conversations in a car, and the nasty Humbert of the novel is beginning to look curiously like a victim.

Carrying flowers and coughing, Humbert arrives at a hospital wherein Lolita, according to her nurse, is feeling "much better today." He accompanies the young woman to Lolita's room, wonders pointedly at some notes he finds near the bed, and is chagrined to learn that they belong to the nurse. She lightly rebukes him, and leaves the room. Seconds later, she returns briefly to request that Humbert, who is himself becoming ill, move his car from the staff's parking lot to the visitors'. He puts this request aside long enough to accuse Lolita of trading the "crummiest of confessions" with her, to present Lolita with three books, and to make an issue over a pair of dark glasses he discovers. Once again, the nurse asks Humbert, brusquely this time, to move his car. He seems annoyed and put-upon. Lolita bids him good-bye, and directs his kiss away from her lips to her cheek, offering the excuse of his cold.

More so than the original, the film illustrates Humbert's paranoia, and injects his parting from Lolita with greater drama. Paranoia is not unknown to the fictional Humbert, who, like his film double, mistakes the nurse's love notes for billets-doux that some unknown admirer has sent to his nymphet (*Lolita* 244–45). But whereas the book is more able to impart his state of mind through straight commentary—

> All at once it occurred to me that her illness was somehow the development of a theme—that it had the same taste and tone as the series of linked impressions which had puzzled and tormented me during our journey; I imagined that secret agent, or secret lover, or prankster, or hallucination, or whatever he was, prowling around the hospital—[243]

the film is more driven to employ objective correlatives. Hence it gives us Humbert's comment about exchanging confessions and his inquiry about the glasses. Because his behavior in the film is more overtly addled, the text more pleadingly solicits our sympathy. This man is not only physically sick, the film shows us, but psychologically wasted; he deserves our indulgence. In the novel, he is led away from Lolita by the nurse; as he passes through the doors, Lolita reminds him to bring her the "new gray suitcase and Mother's trunk" (246). How much more tender is the film, which offers a close-up of the girl's lovely, softly illuminated face; has her say "good-bye" and nothing less firm; and causes her to turn away from Humbert's final kiss. In this myth about love, the moment is critical, and Kubrick refuses to let us overlook it.

That night, as Humbert sleeps under a gigantic pile of blankets in a bleak little cottage, he receives a phone call. Hacking and shivering, he is by now quite ill. We recognize the caller's voice as Quilty's—but he does not identify himself to Humbert. Mockingly, he asks if Humbert is enjoying his stay in town, mentions nebulous rumors about Humbert and his "remarkable" girl, and expresses an interest in Humbert's sex life, noting that Humbert is classified, in some imaginary file, as a "white widowed male." No such phone call occurs in the novel, and its effect here is to continue painting Humbert as victim, and Quilty as villain. The scene prods us to admit that Quilty's methods are gratuitously sadistic, and that Humbert's shortcomings are, by this cold light, comparatively minor. The phrase "white widowed male," incidentally, appears both in the novel's foreword (5) and in various psychiatric case histories (Appel 321).

Agitated, Humbert drives in the dead of night to the hospital, intent on taking Lolita home with him. A nurse-receptionist named Fromkiss indicates that he must first obtain permission from a doctor, prompting Humbert to ask if the facility is a prison or a hospital. She insists that he speak with a Dr. Keegy, whom she pages, and forbids Humbert from going to Lolita's room. When Keegy joins them, he and Fromkiss determine that Lolita was discharged earlier that evening; this surprising fact is confirmed by Lolita's own nurse, Mary, who happens by. Outraged, Humbert bolts toward Lolita's room, and the others move to intercept him. When Humbert attempts to throttle Mary, Keegy and two orderlies manhandle him. Mary explains that Lolita was entrusted to the care of her "uncle," news that detonates another burst of violence from Humbert, who is now flung by the three men to the floor. In the face of Keegy's threat to call the police, Humbert, held flat on his back, calms himself. To appease his assailants, he claims to have forgotten about his brother Gus, who supposedly had arranged to take Lolita with him. Humbert agrees with an orderly's charge that he is "drunk," and adds that he is beset by personal problems. The men lift him to his feet, a haggard, pathetic figure, and escort him to the door.

The projection of Humbert as victim, as someone more sinned against than sinning, reaches its apogee with this scene. In the novel, he learns by telephone that Lolita has been spirited away:

> A bright voice informed me that yes, everything was fine, my daughter had checked out the day before, around two, her uncle, Mr. Gustave, ... had paid Dolly's bill in cash, and told them to tell me I should not worry, and keep warm, they were at Grandpa's ranch as agreed [*Lolita* 248].

The dramatic impact of this message is twice weakened: by Nabokov's imposition of the phone, which denies us the excitement of a face-to-face encounter, and by his conveyance of the moment to the reader indirectly, not representationally. Apprised that Lolita is gone, the fictional Humbert rushes to the hospital where he finds himself "trying to beat up the doctor, and roaring at people under chairs, and clamoring for Mary who luckily for her [is] not there" (248). The action is described very concisely and—again—indirectly; its drama is limited, as is our sense that Humbert is being wantonly used by fate. But Kubrick not only wrings every drop of drama from the scene that he reasonably can, he does so in a manner that causes us to ache for Humbert. The protagonist's health, in the novel, is rebounding (248); in the film, he looks and sounds more like a patient than a visitor. In the novel, he seems neither to win nor to lose the melee (248–49); in the film, he is overpowered and utterly humbled—the camera hovers over his ashen face, and even the music seems to weep for him. A nonoccurrence in the book, his long, slow walk to the exit is masterfully drawn out; the orderlies gently tidy him up, and his valediction is sorrowful: "[Lolita] didn't by any chance leave any message for me? No, I suppose not." The rhetoric of the scene compels us, if not to like Humbert, at least to feel his pain and his loss.

Finale

Leaping ahead to some indeterminate point in the future, the film vouchsafes us a restricted view of a letter being typed. We see only the wide, white expanse of the paper, and the words spasmodically taking shape upon it. Dated March 19 (no year), the letter reads:

> Dear Dad,
> How's everything? I have gone through much sadness and hardship. I'm married. I'm going to have a baby. I'm going nuts because we don't have enough to pay our debts and get out of here. Please send us a check....

The typing continues, but the screen blacks out.

From the standpoint of the novel, the sudden advance to Lolita's letter elides some 20 pages of material. Included in these pages are three packets of information whose absence from the film both tightens the narrative and affects its meaning. First, the fictional Humbert, grief-stricken at the loss of Lolita, retraces his path from Elphinstone, where she vanishes, to Kasbeam. Over a period of months, he registers at 342 hotels, motels, and tourist homes, collecting esoteric clues about his shadow that Quilty has deliberately planted (*Lolita* 250). The elimination of this section, a passage wonderfully entertaining to the reader with a penchant for literary trivia, protects viewers from being shanghaied to an intellectual country where some may feel impatient and uncomfortable. Second, Humbert spends part of a winter and most of the following spring in a familiar Quebec sanatorium, receiving therapy on his "cracking" mind (257). As elsewhere, the film treats him as eccentric and obsessive, but apparently sane, making it easier for viewers to identify with him, and keeping the final cinematic product less barbed. Third, feeling a need for "company and care," Humbert becomes involved with a woman named Rita, whom he picks up "one depraved May evening ... at a darkishly burning bar" (260). He travels with this "sweetest, simplest, gentlest, dumbest Rita imaginable" for no less than two years, from the summer of 1950 to the summer of 1952 (260). Her erasure from the narrative encourages us to construct Lolita as Humbert's only female interest, to fancy that he has devoted his every waking hour to thinking of her, and to take satisfaction in the constancy his dream—which is to say, of his love.

Lolita's letter, what we get of it, is an artful abridgment of the one in the novel (*Lolita* 268). For the film, its word count tumbles from about 150 to about 40. The melancholy tone holds, and is even intensified by the omission of the hilarious line, in reference to her current unpleasant surroundings: "You can't see the morons for the smog" (268). That we are privy to the letter's creation, but not to Humbert's receipt of it—an inversion of what happens in the novel—seems an equal trade-off dramatically. The letter's function does not change: in either text, it allows Humbert to relocate Lolita, and, by contacting her, to press the story to its finish.

Relying still on the trusty station wagon, Humbert drives to a small, wood-frame house, evidently on the outskirts of a city. Before leaving the car, he puts a gun in his coat pocket. He knocks on the door, and is greeted by the pregnant Lolita, now Mrs. Richard T. Schiller. Blandly conciliatory, she invites him in and offers refreshment, which he declines. He notices "Dick" moving about in the back yard, and steps menacingly in his direction, but pulls back when he realizes that Dick is not the man with whom she absconded from the hospital. Humbert demands to know that person's name, and Lolita, swayed by Humbert's promise of money, finally reveals it: Clare Quilty. She explains that she had had a "crush" on Quilty for some time, and regarded him as a genius. Her connection with Dick is somewhat superficial, she admits, and refuses to characterize her former relationship with Humbert. She goes on to recall that Quilty took her to a dude ranch near Santa Fe, but when he asked her to participate in an "art movie," she resisted, and he then expelled her from his circle.

Now Dick and neighbor Bill Crest enter, and, after introductions, Dick and Humbert converse stiffly. Dick unfolds his plan to take

Lolita to Alaska, where they will make a home; the plan is contingent, of course, on Humbert's financial aid. Soon Dick and Bill return to their labors out back, and Humbert chooses this moment to deliver an impassioned speech to Lolita. "Life is very short," he begins; she must give up her pedestrian life with Dick and come away with Humbert. She considers this notion "crazy," and reasons that she has ruined too many chapters in her life to betray Dick now. Sobbing uncontrollably, Humbert presents her with $400 in cash, a check for $2,500, and a mortgage document worth another $10,000. She apologizes for having "cheated" so much, but guesses that such is the "way things are." When she lightly touches his hand, he stands up and, overcome, hurries out the front door to his car, leaving her to call inanely after him: "Let's keep in touch, huh? I'll write you when we get to Alaska."

This lengthy and climactic scene is derived from Chapter 29, Part Two of the novel. Though plentiful, the differences between the texts that crop up through this sequence tend to be modest, and to produce just middling effects. The fictional Lolita's appearance, for example, has, after three years, more obviously altered: she is measurably taller than before, "hugely" pregnant, her gray eyes "washed-out" (*Lolita* 271–74). As the action develops, she smokes, snacks, and indeed plies Humbert with marshmallows and potato chips (273–75). The dollar amount conferred by her stepfather is less spectacular (280–82). From these trifles one infers, respectively, that a character's looks are more easily regulated in prose than in pictures; that the business of smoking and eating, especially the latter, may distract from a drama; and that Humbert's increased generosity is meant to imply greater sacrifice, deeper love.

In a few instances, the film's independence reveals a tad more about the medium's nature and about Kubrick's design. The fictional Humbert understands through a kind of *satori* that Dick is not his enemy (*Lolita* 273). In the film, however, Humbert's attack on him is forestalled by Lolita's words; it is an adaptive strategy that bares Humbert's mental processes to the audience, and moreover leads the two principals to interact. In the novel, when Humbert badgers Lolita to disclose her secret friend's name, she does—but only to Humbert, not to the reader:

> "Do you really want to know who it was? Well, it was—"
> And softly, confidentially, arching her thin eyebrows and puckering her parched lips, she emitted, a little mockingly, somewhat fastidiously, not untenderly, in a kind of muted whistle, the name that the astute reader has guessed long ago [273–74].

The trick keeps the novel something of a detective story for the less "astute" reader; by contrast, the film, with its spotlight on Quilty, is a detective story for Humbert alone. Perhaps most arresting is a moment when, in the novel, Humbert has given Lolita his *cadeau*, and has implored her once again to leave with him. She responds: "No, it is quite out of the question. I would sooner go back to [Quilty]" (281). The deletion of this untoward comparison saves the film *Lolita* a dram of polish, and enables us to care more for her and for Humbert, both of whom are made to seem worthier. With some consistency, the film appeals more than the novel to our conventional expectations, less to the dark side of our imagination.

Having disposed of Lolita's decision to remain with Dick, the film is liberated now to flow rapidly to its conclusion. Humbert drives through a swirling fog, and presently steps into Quilty's bric-a-brac-strewn mansion. As at the start of the film, he calls out Quilty's name, but this time the screen goes to black, and soon fills with the bullet-ripped portrait of the young girl, the flimsy shield behind which Quilty attempts to save himself from Humbert's frontier justice. Accompanied by mournful music, an epilog scrolls; it reads simply: "Humbert Humbert died of coronary thrombosis in prison awaiting trial for the murder of Clare Quilty." The closing credits are minimal.

Like the rest of the film, its ending demonstrates respect for the original, yet discovers its own means of expression. As Kristin Thompson (citing Shklovsky) reminds us, it is not uncommon for a narrative's ending to make reference to its beginning (40), but both the film and the novel carry this tendency to an extreme. The fictional foreword and the story proper begin with the same word—"Lolita"—which also caps the text. Further, Humbert's first paragraph and his last share the same wild tone: one of poetry, rapture, epiphany. Emphasizing murder and revenge, and avoiding the more delicate issue of sexuality, the film begins and ends not with Lolita but with Quilty. Yet by forming a kind of narrational loop in which the ending feeds directly back into the beginning, the film actually outdoes its source, and recalls the circular structure of *Finnegans Wake*, authored, perhaps not coincidentally, by one of Nabokov's favorites, the "*sublime Dublinois*" (*Lolita* 209). One also appreciates Kubrick's symbolic use of the portrait. Though he omits any forthright indication of Lolita's future—the fictional character is destined to die giving stillbirth (6)—the painted image of the smiling girl, with its bullet hole through the face, silently speaks not only of Lolita's past and present, but of her days to come. Whatever remains of her life has been irrecoverably marred, partly by her own actions, as she admits, and certainly by the abuses of Quilty and Humbert.

Notwithstanding the myriad changes Kubrick worked in translating *Lolita* from fiction to film, I judge the adaptation to be a faithful one insofar as it captures the letter of the original. (Let me stress that this judgment is intended as a neutral observation, signifying neither approval nor disapproval.) The main characters and events of the novel are, for the most part, still present and recognizable in the film. I must contend, however, that the film is markedly less loyal to the book's irreverent spirit, and on this count I do concede some disappointment. The loss of eroticism, given the social conditions under which the film was produced, was inevitable. Hemmed in as he was, Kubrick here sought to make a virtue of necessity: "In the film," he has stated, "the fact that [Humbert's] sexual obsession could not be portrayed [tends] to imply from the start that he [is] in love with [Lolita]" (Bernstein 79). Narrowly considered, this development is not by itself a cause for regret. But along with the eroticism went much of the original's warped and pulsing energy, its joltingly singular view of life. In an excess of adaptive caution, Kubrick succeeded in domesticating Nabokov's exotic animal, but only by removing its fangs and claws; a great novel was turned into merely a good film.

Chapter 3
The Shining

Published in 1977, *The Shining* was Stephen King's third novel under his own name, following *Carrie* and *'Salem's Lot*; it was his fourth if one counts *Rage,* which he released under the nom de plume Richard Bachman (Beahm 4). *The Shining* is a gothic horror story centering on struggling writer and reformed alcoholic Jack Torrance, his wife Wendy, and their five-year-old psychic boy Danny. Dismissed from his teaching position for beating a student, Jack brings his family to the Overlook, an isolated Colorado resort hotel of which he is to be the winter caretaker. The hotel, of course, is haunted. Over time, Jack's behavior becomes increasingly erratic, and a colorful array of ghosts manifests itself to him and to Danny. When a heavy snow cuts the Torrances off from the outside world, Jack, goaded by evil forces and his own frustrations, becomes violent and attempts to kill his wife and son. But the projected victims prove engagingly resourceful, giving Jack and his supportive apparitions all they can handle. Using telepathy, Danny finally secures help in the form of the hotel's cook, Dick Hallorann. After more strife, Dick, Wendy, and Danny escape the hotel just as its ancient, dyspeptic boiler explodes, destroying the property and killing Jack.

The Shining is what George Orwell, with a nod to G. K. Chesterton, called a "good bad book" (19). He defined this phenomenon as the "kind of book that has no literary pretensions but which remains readable when more serious productions have vanished" (19). Although the intellect refuses to accord it much respect, such a book may amuse or excite or even move the reader (21). Like the rest of King's extensive oeuvre, *The Shining* is perforated with technical and artistic deficiencies. The narrative is overburdened with flashbacks that retard its pace and bootlessly rehash the same material (Ball 21). The punctuation and capitalization frequently descend to comic strip level, as in *"???WHAT PARTY???"* and *"????WHAT MASKS????"* (*Shining* 298). Though some of the imagery is adroit and effective, much of it is ludicrous. At one point, Jack has terror in the "back of his throat like a taste of gone-over cherries" (254). He advises his wife that she has truths "knocking around up in [her] head like a bunch of loose cue balls. [She needs] to shoot them into the pockets" (261). Hurrying along in his Buick, Dick "squeeze[s] the accelerator like the breast of a much-loved woman" (385). Here and there, participles dangle like broken limbs:

> Danny had called for Mr. Hallorann, and upstairs, sitting next to Danny in fear ..., that had seemed like the faintest of all hopes. But standing here, ... it seemed almost possible [365].

King's fondness for clichés, brand-name references (meant to build verisimilitude), and slapdash interior monolog is profusely displayed throughout the text. But while these problems may dishearten the academic, they do not necessarily impede the filmmaker. To the contrary, if Nabokov's *Lolita* conceivably intimidated some potential adapters with its gleaming literary merit (Max 130), no such stigma could be affixed to *The Shining*.

As the oxymoron "good bad" implies, however, *The Shining* has favorable qualities that go beyond its lack of pretense, and its special appeal to Stanley Kubrick is easy enough to fathom. The major characters, while not deep, are rendered in ample detail; perhaps more importantly, they are pictured internally as well as externally, providing Kubrick with the psychological bearings he always desires (Kubrick 306). Certainly the narrative is filled with action, some of it riotous—yet it is also veiled with the gauzy ambiguity, the obliqueness, that Kubrick takes as a means of advancing the truth (306). Colin Westerbeck speculated that the director was fascinated by the stark mise-en-scène of the hotel, which is so huge, empty, and imposing, much like the settings that dominate *2001: A Space Odyssey* (439). Then too, Kubrick has frankly acknowledged his attraction to "supernatural" stories and to "ghost" stories (Houston 44). In this vein, one must admit that, regardless of King's weaknesses as a writer, he does have a particular knack that seldom flags: he is "able to convince the reader that the unreal is actually occurring" (Kanfer 21). Kubrick himself has partially explained his interest in King's novel by citing its metaphysical aspect:

> There's something inherently wrong with the human personality. There's an evil side to it. One of the things that horror stories can do is show us the archetypes of the unconscious: we can see the dark side without having to confront it directly. Also, ghost stories appeal to our craving for immortality. If you can be afraid of a ghost, then you have to believe that a ghost may exist. And if a ghost exists, then oblivion might not be the end [Kroll, "Horror" 99].

King's first of many hardcover best-sellers (Beahm 11), the novel was generally well received by critics. Although some had misgivings about the author's mechanics (Ball 21; Bannon 52; *Booklist* 992; Lingeman 35; Sullivan 8), most of them agreed that he had created a worthy exemplum of the horror genre. John Ball, for instance, declared it a "real chiller" (21); *Kirkus Reviews* found it "back-prickling" (1277); and even Richard Lingeman, who deplored the fumblings of King's style, felt obliged to admit that the tale "serves up the scary stuff with unremitting dexterity" (35).

Although Kubrick's film had its defenders, it was by and large met with a critical antipathy that seems sometimes to have verged on seething resentment. A recurrent note in the critics' indignation is one that gets sounded routinely in carping discussions of the adaptive art: the claim that the director has tampered recklessly and contrarily with a presumably sacrosanct preexisting work. Impressed with King's "mesmerizing, terrifying" novel (80), Henry Bromell had hoped that the film would make him feel "sick, giddy, thrilled" (81); he was instead puzzled to encounter not a horror film, but what he deemed a lame parody of one (82). John Simon, who had not read the novel, was nonetheless sadly convinced that Kubrick had "played fast and loose" with the original story ("Visu" 795). Suffering a like reaction, *Variety*'s reviewer was appalled that Kubrick had, by personal estimate, dispensed with no less than "90 percent of King's creation to concentrate on Jack Nicholson" (14). These sentiments were echoed again by Richard Jameson, who accused the director of eliminating "most" of King's fantastic inventions, and withholding "virtually all" of Jack Torrance's mottled history—changes that, in his view, crippled the film (29). Stanley Kauffmann administered what was probably the unkindest cut of all when he wrote: "*The Shining* doesn't scare" ("Dulling" 27). Across the critical divide, those few rebels who cheered the film relished the new and subtle counterpoise between the natural and the supernatural (Hatch 733; Kroll, "Horror" 96; Schickel 69), and, as is common with Kubrick, his visual elegance.

Paralleling what happened with Nabokov and *Lolita*, King's opinion of Kubrick's adaptation seems to have deteriorated with time. In *Danse Macabre,* published in 1981, King wrote: "Three of my novels have [to date] been released as films: *Carrie* ..., *'Salem's Lot* ..., and *The Shining* ..., and in all three cases I feel that I have been fairly treated" (207). But by 1983 his public assessment of Kubrick's efforts on *The Shining* had become sharply critical. This second set of remarks goes to the core of adaptation as a problem, and is therefore reproduced at some length:

> I'm still profoundly ambivalent about the whole thing. I'd admired Kubrick for a long time and had great expectations for the project, but I was deeply disappointed in the end result. Parts of the film are chilling, charged with a relentlessly claustrophobic terror, but others fall flat.
>
> I think there are two basic problems with the movie. First, Kubrick is a very cold man—pragmatic and rational—and he had great difficulty conceiving, even academically, of a supernatural world.... [A] visceral skeptic such as Kubrick just couldn't grasp the sheer inhuman evil of the Overlook Hotel. So he looked, instead, for evil in the characters and made the film into a domestic tragedy with only vaguely supernatural overtones. That was the basic flaw: because he couldn't believe, he couldn't make the film believable to others.
>
> The second problem was in characterization and casting. Jack Nicholson, though a fine actor, was all wrong for the part. His last big role had been in *One Flew over the Cuckoo's Nest,* and between that and his manic grin, the audience automatically identified him as a loony from the first scene. But the book is about Jack Torrance's

gradual *descent* into madness through the malign influence of the Overlook.... If the guy is nuts to begin with, then the entire tragedy of his downfall is wasted. For that reason, the film has no center and no heart.... What's basically wrong with Kubrick's version of *The Shining* is that it's a film by a man who thinks too much and feels too little; and that's why, for all its virtuoso effects, it never gets you by the throat and hangs on the way real horror should [*Playboy* Interview 23–24].

In my judgment, the criticisms mounted by King and others against Kubrick's vision are both misguided and overstated. The dogged belief that an adaptation may triumph only by adhering religiously to its source has been debunked countless times. Moreover, much of the vitriol excerpted above seems somewhat hysterical: Is it true, for example, that Kubrick discarded "90 percent" of the original? Is it universally agreed that the film is less believable than the novel, or that it is incapable of inducing a fright in anyone? While one might argue that the film is flawed in ways that the novel is not, the reverse might also be argued with equal or greater conviction. In the end, one's opinion of the texts must remain only an opinion, but the following rhetorical analysis should clarify the basis for any lingering debate.

Exposition

The film begins with a constantly shifting aerial view of Jack's yellow Volkswagen as it motors along a thin, winding ribbon of mountain road. Ominous horn music, interspersed with otherworldly trills and howls, accompanies the opening credits. Presently Jack arrives at his destination, the sprawling, tony Overlook Hotel; inside, he is directed to the office of Stuart Ullman, with whom he has an appointment. Ullman greets him warmly, offering him a chair and coffee.

Differences between the paired texts, modest but meaningful, are announced instantly. Jack's journey to the hotel is not depicted in the novel, which begins *in medias res* with his job interview. As a practical matter, the aerial sequence grants the film a long moment during which it can run its obligatory credits. But the sequence also cleverly serves to prefigure the film's spooky direction. The first eerie throb of music signals that something is amiss, as does the eldritch camera-work:

> Suddenly the camera stops tracking the car and flies out over the landscape. Thus we're told that this isn't a conventional shot in which the camera is supposed to be "invisible" and the emphasis is on the car. Here the emphasis is on the camera, the watcher, a presence of some sort that can follow the car or not as it chooses [Kauffmann, "Dulling" 26].

We are likewise quickly made aware of the hotel's intimidating size, and of its apparent remoteness from the reassuring hubbub of community life. By contrast, the novel tends to insinuate its tone more deliberately—though one does appreciate the epigraphs from Poe and Goya, and the early comparison of Ullman to the "local undertaker" (*Shining* 3). A toadish figure in the book, Ullman has been utterly reinvented for the film: he now radiates charm, grace, gentility. His manner puts us temporarily at ease in these new surroundings, asserting an everyday normality, and brushing aside any shivers caused by the weird preamble.

Abandoning the scene in Ullman's office, the film takes us through a dissolve to an apartment complex. Inside, Danny and Wendy sit eating sandwiches at the kitchen table. He seems fretful about perhaps spending the winter at "that hotel," and yet not pleased to be living where he is: it is taking him a while to "make new friends." His imaginary friend Tony is completely resistant to the prospect of the Overlook, though he declines to say why. Wendy soothingly predicts that if they move to the hotel, they will all enjoy a good time.

This conversation between mother and son is drawn mainly from Chapter 2 of the novel. Having introduced Jack, it is logical that the narrative—either version—promptly give a glimpse of the two remaining central characters. Interestingly, the film tells us less here about the situation than the novel does, and also more. The fictional dialog is longer, and contains more peripheral information. Worried about the well-being of the Volkswagen, Danny uses a vulgarism that brings a half-page admonishment from Wendy (*Shining* 12). More significantly, he asks her to explain why his father lost his job. She answers truthfully that Jack struck a boy named George Hatfield and was consequently fired (13–14). But the only trace evidence in the film that any such upheaval has occurred is Jack's seeking a short-term job, and the suggestion, later confirmed by Wendy, that the family has recently relocated. Kubrick has simplified and condensed the narrative. But he has also provided an early visit with Tony, whom the novel does not establish until Chapter 4. Originally described as a shadowy, subjective figure who appears at the limit of Danny's vision and takes him places (29; 139), Tony is now a bobbing index finger that speaks with Danny's roughened voice; he has become objectified for the screen. One notes, in addition, that the film Danny is watching a *Roadrunner* cartoon on television, another departure from the source; the program hints of life-and-death chases to come.

In Ullman's office, he and Jack are joined by Bill Watson, who will take Jack on a tour of the premises. Continuing the conversation, Jack tags himself as a writer who is "looking for a change." Ullman, plainly convinced that Jack is ideal for the caretaker position, explains that the Overlook is closed down every winter due to the site's inaccessibility in snow, and goes on to outline what will be required of Jack: maintenance and repair of the building. Ullman warns of the sense of isolation that comes with the job, but Jack professes no qualms. Sheepishly, Ullman now reveals a piece of the hotel's history that has been known to unnerve other applicants. In 1970, a caretaker named Grady became afflicted with "cabin fever" and ran amok, killing his wife and two daughters with an ax, stacking their bodies neatly in a room of the west wing, and then shooting himself through the mouth with a double-barreled shotgun. Jack seems unruffled by the tale, and supposes that his wife, a "ghost story and horror film addict," will be fascinated.

As it develops in the novel, the interview is quite similar in its structure and outcome. But the fictional Ullman's grating style, and the resultant tension between him and Jack, tint their discussion a much darker shade. These two men have formed an immediate and astringent dislike for each other. "Officious little prick," Jack thinks, in the novel's first sentence (*Shining* 3); for his part, Ullman lets Jack know that, given a free hand, he would not hire him. But an old friend of Jack's, Al Shockley, who happens to sit on the Board of Directors, has given Ullman no choice (5). Rhetorically, it soon becomes clear that the animosity between Ullman and Jack is tied to a whole deeper layer of the novel: to Jack's drinking escapades with Al at Stovington Preparatory Academy, to Jack's determination to write a book based on the Overlook's checkered past, to his unwillingness (born of ambition, not loyalty) to leave the hotel even when he suspects he should. But since the film cannot, for time constraints, delve into this layer, it follows that the second Ullman must be affable. His affability need not be explained, but his hostility would probably have to be, and the film simply does not have time.

Brushing his teeth, Danny asks Tony if he thinks Jack will get the job. Tony replies that Jack has already gotten it, and will call in a moment to tell Wendy; the phone call comes exactly as forecast. Danny now asks Tony why he would rather not go to the hotel, and Tony, after first resisting, delivers an uncanny vision: a torrent of blood comes spilling out of the hotel's elevator; in another room, two mannequin-like girls stare at us mutely; at the elevator, the deluge of blood continues, rushing at us until it blackens our view. When next we see Danny, he is lying in his bed, being examined by a soft-spoken female physician. He admits having contacted Tony, but otherwise discloses little about him. Consulting privately with Wendy, the doctor doubts that the boy has any serious malady. In response to light but incisive questioning, Wendy admits that Danny did not adjust well to nursery school, that Jack, drunk and angry, once dislocated Danny's shoulder, and that Jack has sworn off alcohol.

This sequence concludes the film's introduction, which corresponds to Part One, or "Prefatory Matters," in the novel. Juxtaposing the texts, one marvels at the masses of information that have been either omitted from the film or reduced to an inkling. In a novel populated by curious characters, Watson may be the most outlandish of all. A "beefy man with fluffy popcorn hair" (*Shining* 17), he babbles crudely and incessantly when showing Jack the boiler, lending the book its only real humor. Watson summarizes Ullman, and his relationship to Ullman, thus:

Yap-yap-yap, all the livelong day, he's just like one a those little dogs that bites you on the ankle then run around an [*sic*] pee all over the rug. If brains was black powder he couldn't blow his own nose. It's a pity the things you see when you ain't got a gun [19].

By dropping this episode, and by making Watson into a slight, sepulchral sort who barely speaks, the film heightens its air of foreboding, and sidesteps thorny questions about Ullman. Most of the other omissions pertain to Jack. The novel recounts his drinking bouts in Vermont, bouts that nearly wreck his marriage (41–42), but that give him a valuable ally in Al Shockley. (Jack and Al jointly forswear drinking after a near catastrophe they share one woozy night on the highway [38–40].) Jack's legitimate credentials as a writer—he once sold a short story to *Esquire* (48)—are also detailed. In disposing of this texture, Kubrick speeds his project, but whittles down the fullness of King's story. Transformed, it is already becoming elliptical, mysterious.

The scenes that do get presented round out the film's exposition. All the preliminary data (or all that Kubrick warrants necessary) are now slid into place so that the narrative may ascend to its next level of action, at the Overlook: Danny is demonstrably psychic; Jack has won the job; and, not long ago, he exhibited destructive behavior toward his family. Again, however, the film's narrational strategy differs noticeably from that of its source. Whereas the film Danny's fearful intuition does not directly involve his father, the fictional Danny's does. In the novel, when Jack comes home from the interview, Danny sees, on the front seat of the car, a "short-handled mallet, its head clotted with blood and hair. Then it [is] just a bag of groceries" (*Shining* 34). Later, Danny remembers a dream in which his father hurts him (43). By raising our fears, but pointing them away from Jack, the film operates in this case with greater subtlety than the book. The visit from the doctor actually originates in Chapter 17, when a Dr. Edmonds checks Danny for epilepsy, watches him plunge into a psychic trance, then decides that Danny has no more than "unusually keen" perception (137–47). Transposing the visit to the start of the tale is both a cause and an effect of the quickened pace. Of course, the discussion with the doctor also furnishes a chance to apprise the viewer of Jack's sometime instability. In the novel, Wendy silently *recalls* his behavior; that technique inconvenient for him, Kubrick devises a nimble alternative.

Closing Day

Negotiating the familiar, serpentine road, Jack drives his family toward the Overlook. He is faintly scowling as the scene begins, and the others' attempts to communicate with him are curtly rebuffed. He does become a tad more responsive when Danny asks him to explain Wendy's reference to the "Donner party." The scowl melts gradually into a strange smile as Jack speaks of the legendary settlers who became snowbound in the mountains, and, to survive, resorted to cannibalism.

A variant of the novel's Chapter 8, this scene twists and exaggerates certain tendencies therein. The fictional Jack, too, is somewhat grumpy. As the aged Volkswagen labors up Sidewinder Pass, Wendy worries aloud about the fitful fuel pump. "'The fuel pump will go another three miles,' Jack [says] shortly" (*Shining* 62). Looking ahead to their arrival at the Overlook, he mutters: "That goddam Ullman better still be up there. I guess he is" (63). But these two comments represent only one facet of his mood, which is in fact mutable. At the chapter's start, Jack feels playful enough to fondle Wendy's leg, not once but repeatedly (61); later, he absorbs the vista of the hotel, set in its "wide square of green lawn," with a tranquil reflectiveness (64). The film's emphasis on his irritability points to a condensation of events, intimating that some malignant influence is already at work on him: that he is already beginning to change. Similarly, in the novel it is Wendy who silently muses—but says nothing—about the Donner party (62). But by allowing Jack to hold forth as he does, the film casts a lurid light on him. Why, we are nudged to wonder, does he take such apparent (and unholy) pleasure in discussing cannibalism with his little boy?

At the Overlook, Ullman proposes to give Jack and Wendy a tour, while Danny busies himself in the game room. Ullman leads the Torrances through the Colorado Lounge, where he notes that the Indian motif in the decor is authentic, and that the hotel has had an "illustrious past." Meanwhile Danny, throwing darts, receives a second visitation from the look-alike girls in their blue party dresses. In the staff wing, Ullman shows Jack and Wendy their quarters, which Jack pronounces "cozy" and "homey." Outside, Ullman walks them by the hedge maze and the Sno-Cat; he mentions that the hotel was built on an Indian burial ground. Back inside, the group enters the Gold Ball Room, whose bar has been stripped of its liquor, a circumstance that moves Jack to volunteer: "We don't drink." Dick Hallorann, the hotel chef, is introduced, and a woman ushers in Danny, who, she reports, had been outside searching for his parents.

Just as the narrative as a whole has an exposition, so does this phase of the narrative. We are offered, along with Jack and Wendy, an orientation to the Overlook that touches on its appearance, history, and layout. This sequence is inspired largely by the novel's Chapter 12, in which Ullman shows all three Torrances much of the hotel's interior, including the Presidential Suite and their humble but livable apartment (*Shining* 93–98). In the film, Danny's separation from the others makes his parents seem a trifle thoughtless, and adds some weight to the critical contention that Kubrick's project is as much a tragedy of the family as an adventure in supernatural horror (Harvey 64–65; Hatch 732; Westerbeck 439). The fictional topiary hedges, clipped into a menagerie of assorted animals that come menacingly to life ("an insoluble special-effects problem," Jameson supposed [29]), are replaced by a labyrinth of very tall but stationary hedges that will figure in the film's climax. Jack's statement about not drinking is bound up in his character and in the plot, and is duly carried over from the book, although originally he says: "*I* don't drink" (emphasis added), and addresses the line to Dick (*Shining* 78). Ullman's revelation that the Overlook was erected on an Indian burial ground is not found in the source, and is, as John Simon observed, puzzling, since none of the eventual specters is an Indian ("Visu" 796); the reference is either an intentional "red herring," (Schickel 69), or a solecism in the film's rhetoric: it goes nowhere.

A gentle, friendly black man, Dick takes Wendy and Danny to see the kitchen and associated facilities. So cavernous is the kitchen that Wendy jokes about having to leave a trail of bread crumbs every time she enters it. Now Dick opens the door to the walk-in freezer and cheerfully tabulates its contents. In the course of his banter, he twice calls Danny by his family nickname of "Doc"; when Wendy asks how he has come to know this private appellation, Dick is pleasantly evasive. Next, he shows her the storage room, in which dried and canned goods are kept. While detailing what these goods are, he asks Danny a question telepathically: "How'd you like some ice cream, Doc?" Soon after, Wendy departs with Jack, Ullman, and Watson, leaving Danny alone with Dick.

Modeled closely on the events of Chapter 10, the film's tour through the kitchen is still recognizably different. In the novel, Jack is a part of the group; "out of his element," he stays in the background and speaks only occasionally (*Shining* 72). His absence from the film tour costs the sequence nothing dramatically. Indeed, the magnetic presence of Jack Nicholson would have tended to arrogate our attention, and would have compromised the purity of the situation: the three "good" characters are together by themselves, giving us a glimpse of common virtue in action. Two other items underscore the film's craft. In the novel, Dick mentally asks Danny if he would like to accompany Dick to Florida (74). By substituting a question about ice cream, the film smoothly sets up their forthcoming exchange about shining in a way that the original question does not. Also, the novel has Danny match Dick's ability to intuit a name. Having guessed that Danny is called "Doc," Dick pretends to have forgotten his own name. Danny, who has never heard Dick's first name spoken, grins and fills in the ostensible blank: "Mr. Hallorann. Dick, to your friends" (75). This one-upmanship would have seemed ham-handed in the film (as perhaps it is in the book), and the fact that the two share a special power is conveyed adequately without it.

A bowl of chocolate ice cream in front of him, Danny listens quietly as Dick explains the mystery of "shining," or extrasensory perception. The boy seems reluctant to talk about it, and advises Dick that Tony has ruled it a taboo topic. When Dick asks about Tony, Danny briefly describes him, and admits that Tony unaccountably "tells" him things.

Obviously Tony has alerted Danny that something about the Overlook is to be feared. Dick pooh-poohs any cause for alarm, allowing that some of what has transpired in the hotel over the years has been unfortunate, and has left behind "traces" that people who shine can detect. Danny indicates that he is particularly concerned about Room 237. Startled, Dick asserts that the room contains nothing unusual, but orders Danny to stay out of it anyway, an injunction he forcefully repeats.

This scene deviates from the original in some ways that matter, and in some that do not. The fictional conversation takes place in Dick's parked Plymouth Fury, not in the hotel's kitchen (*Shining* 80); the number of the bothersome room is 217, not 237 (87). Such changes have no measurable effect on how we interpret the story. On the other hand, one notices that the novel's dialog is much more expansive and far-ranging than the film's. Cutting it, which is almost a necessity in view of a child actor's limited capacity to master lines, saves time. But the minimalist give-and-take of the film, especially on Danny's part, comes to nurture a terrible apprehension that much is going unsaid; the want of words speaks as loudly as the words themselves, and creates suspense. The original Dick has Danny test his telepathic strength, and discovers—painfully—that he is a veritable "pistol" (83). Dick suggests that if trouble does develop, Danny should contact him mentally in Florida (89), and the evidence of Danny's vigor makes such a contact plausible. In eliminating this by-play, the film is less blunt about a potential means of rescue—yet the chance that Danny could reach Dick has been implied regardless. But perhaps the most significant adjustment to the passage is its new placement in the narrative. In the novel, the conversation is followed by Ullman's grand tour, and then by a limp little chapter in which the Torrances stand on the front porch and watch the leaves whirl and skitter across the lawn (101); the segment just dwindles and fades. But in the film, Dick's stern warning disquiets us; and then, with a jolt, the narrative hurtles ahead. The film seeks, and locates, a drama that eludes the book.

The Crisis Foreshadowed

This next section of the film corresponds to Part Three of the novel, titled "The Wasps' Nest." In either text, we are confronted at this stage with a steadily accumulating mound of evidence that the trouble dimly foreseen by the fictional Dick is now emerging. Jack's thinking becomes obscure, his behavior erratic, and the others grow leery of him. But the process whereby these effects are achieved is grossly different from text to text. Any resemblances between the paired segments are almost wholly atmospheric, not substantive, and those critics who have decried the film tend to recall this rupture in the story lines as a chief source of their discontent. If King spends almost too long inside Jack's imploding mind, examining its fissures with minute and even tiresome care, Kubrick stays outside, giving us snatches of Jack's physical and social aberrance exclusively. Virtually a story unto itself, what Kubrick omits from the sequence enables the film to maintain its comparative fleetness, but at some price in clarity; the trade-off is a touchy one.

A month has passed. Somewhere in the mountains a coyote sings a grim aubade as Wendy trundles breakfast out of the kitchen and across the Colorado Lounge. At the same time, Danny zooms his tricycle through the halls. Wendy enters the bedroom and gently awakens Jack with the food; he is amazed to hear it is eleven thirty. Although he has no viable ideas, he supposes he should attempt to write after eating. He claims to love the Overlook, and adds that he felt acquainted with it from the outset, as if he had been here before. Later in the day, his typewriter sits unused while he hurls a tennis ball against a wall of the Lounge, catching it and hurling it back again. Outside, Wendy teasingly chases Danny, who leads her into the blind alleys of the maze, where they struggle to find their way. Jack soon becomes bored with throwing the ball, and drifts over to a miniature replica of the maze; peering down into it, he sees, or seems to see, his wife and son strolling about in its midst.

Apart from the many radical changes that Kubrick institutes—to be discussed separately and belatedly—one appreciates some smaller refinements as well. In the sequence limned above, we encounter, for example, further signs of compression. At the start of the novel's Part Three, Jack is productive in both his caretaking and his writing. Though proceeding at a leisurely pace, he is in fact shingling the Overlook's roof, and finding peace in the activity

(*Shining* 105–6). He is likewise progressing well with his play, *The Little School,* having outlasted a period of writer's block (106–7). The Jack of the film, however, seems not only unproductive but entropic—the few actions he musters are negative. Without any delay, his madness is creeping upon him.

Two other adaptive flourishes bear notice, the first of which works more successfully than the second. The fictional Danny walks and sometimes runs through the hotel (see, for instance, *Shining* 169–74). Putting the film Danny on a tricycle and then tracking him with a Steadicam is a small but heady triumph of filmmaking. As Jameson noted,

> the action is punctuated with one of those vivid, lushly particular moment-of-cinematic-discovery effects that has virtually an atavistic appeal: the clump-*whoosh*, clump-*whoosh* sound as the child trikes, with blithe relentlessness, across the polished floor and deep-piled carpet [30].

Every turn in his brisk route is a climax, a bubble of fear that bursts only to reform a moment later. Jack's peering down into the scale-model maze and apparently seeing his family is more problematic. The effect is dazzling but confusing, and calls up a long series of nettlesome questions: Is the shot simply a fancy segue from one scene to the next? Or does Jack actually behold Wendy and Danny in the toy maze? If so, by what mechanism are they there? Why does he not react to this miracle? Or is he merely projecting their image by dint of imagination (Jameson 30)? If he is somehow gazing down into the real maze, how is the view possible? Moreover, what does the shot mean? It would seem to suggest that Jack is vaguely in league with the spirit of the Overlook (Jameson 30), yet the awesome power that the shot imports is belied by his sheer incompetence as a villain, and by his ultimate defeat. The scene has no precedent in the novel, and appears to be rhetoric gone awry.

A title tells us it is now Tuesday. In the kitchen, Wendy prepares a meal while listening to the news on television. The newswoman mentions a man who is serving a life sentence for shooting someone, and an Aspen woman who disappeared while on a hunting trip with her husband. According to the weatherman, a snowstorm will strike tomorrow. Once again Danny peddles his tricycle through the endless corridors of the hotel. On impulse, he stops near Room 237 and, with a mixture of fear and bravery, tries the door; it is locked. We get another glimpse of the ghostly girls before Danny scoots away. In the Colorado Lounge, Jacks types like an automaton until Wendy, hoping to chat, interrupts him. His mood quickly degenerates from irascibility to barely contained fury. He commands her never to bother him when he is in the Lounge, and harshly dismisses her. Thursday sees Wendy and Danny frolicking in the snow; inside, an unkempt Jack stands and stares blankly, a fire at his back.

Although much of this material is newly invented, some of it has been transferred from the novel and altered in the process. Drawn by a "morbid kind of curiosity" (*Shining* 169), the fictional Danny makes his own preliminary visit to the forbidden room, but his undertaking seems more protracted, more complicated. Consuming almost six pages of Chapter 19, the adventure begins with Danny's recollection of the Bluebeard myth, in which the ogre's wife is proscribed from looking inside a certain room (169–70). Danny hesitates while mulling over the myth, then finds his passkey, pauses again—for "several minutes" (170)—slips the key into the lock, but then withdraws it and walks away (171). Retreating, he becomes terrified by a fire extinguisher whose brass nozzle suddenly thumps to the carpet (172). After another lengthy bout of paralysis, he makes himself run to the stairs as he imagines the snakelike hose slithering after him (173–74). The film's version of this episode is shorter, sharper, and yet no less frightening; the flash of the girls is not unlike the thump of the nozzle. Jack's behavior is also rooted in the novel, though the context differs. Poring over a scrapbook he has discovered in the basement, the fictional Jack acts guilty when Wendy intrudes on him: he reflexively hides the book (165), much as the film Jack yanks out the sheet of typing paper and conceals it. In either setting, he seems to have been caught, or nearly caught, misbehaving. Antecedents for his eruptive temper also exist in the novel, to wit, his angry shouts when Danny locks himself in the bathroom (124–26), and when the family is attacked by a swarm of wasps (132–36). The specific model for Jack's ugly screen exchange with Wendy appears to be an incident in which he contracts a headache at the local library. Hoping that she might give him some Excedrin, he is annoyed to learn she can supply him with nothing but Anacin. "Want some water?" she asks brightly. *"No," he thinks, "I just want you to GET THE FUCK OUT OF HERE!"* (177). In the film, his enmity is verbalized, making it seem all the more severe.

On Saturday, the snow thickens, and Wendy learns that the telephone is inoperative. Using the hotel's CB radio, she contacts the Forest Service, and is advised that many of the lines are down—probably until spring. Elsewhere, Danny rounds a corner on his tricycle; he is petrified to see the undead girls blocking his way. In unison, they extend him an invitation: "Hello, Danny. Come and play with us. Come and play with us, Danny, for ever and ever and ever." They seem to advance on him as they speak, and at times appear to him tossed in blood-spattered death, a monstrous ax lying in the foreground. The girls vanish, and Tony reminds him that they are not real in any event. On Monday, Danny obtains his mother's permission to go to his room and retrieve his fire engine; she instructs him to move quietly since his father went to bed just a "few hours ago." As it happens, Jack is not asleep, but sitting on the side of the bed staring into space. When Danny passes by, Jack stirs, and stuporously asks Danny to join him. Danny climbs meekly into his lap, and they have an offish, halting conversation in which Jack reaffirms that he loves the hotel—he wishes they could stay here "for ever and ever and ever"—and Danny betrays an anxiety that Jack might harm him or Wendy. Jack seems paranoid about Wendy, but assures his son that he loves him, and would never hurt him. His jouncing eyebrows and maniacal leer, however, argue otherwise.

Coordination between the texts continues to be weak through here. Danny's interlude with the murdered girls originates in the novel's Chapter 34. Exploring the snowdrifted playground one afternoon, Danny digs his way into an igloo-like jungle gym (*Shining* 285). He begins to feel he is no longer alone (286), and, panicked, he studies from a distance the

> fold of shadow that mark[s] the hole he'd dug to get down inside. Now, in spite of the snow-dazzle, he [thinks] he [can] see something

there. Something moving. A hand. The waving hand of some desperately unhappy child, waving hand, pleading hand, drowning hand.

(Save me O please save me If you can't save me at least come play with me ... Forever. And Forever. And Forever.) [288]

From such a tiny and rather unpromising seed has Kubrick fashioned the recurrent imagery of the ghost-girls, who, in the novel, are never actually pictured. But Kubrick pictures them not only in life but in gory death; his turn is toward the physical, the visual, and results in an amplified horror.

Danny's strained conversation with Jack has a hazy progenitor in Chapter 16. Recovering from a frightening experience with Tony, the fictional Danny asks his father to linger with him "for a minute," a phrase Jack uses in the film (*Shining* 127). Their ensuing dialog is laced with items that do not survive condensation: references to a Snoopy night-light, the game of roque, the puzzle of "redrum" (128). Those items that do survive make up the keystones of the film exchange: Jack asks if Danny is "okay," denies that he would hurt Danny or Wendy, and concludes by whispering: "I love you, Danny. God knows I do" (127–29). Despite these parallels, the ambiance of the film is bleaker and more portentous. In the film, Danny is lucid while Jack is out of sorts; in the novel, these poles are reversed. In the film, Danny's concern about his and Wendy's safety brings a delusional train from Jack: "Did your mother ever say that to you? That I would hurt you?" Though rattled, the fictional Jack harbors no duplicate suspicions about his wife. Most glaringly, the film Jack echoes the words of the two girls, wishing that the family might remain at the hotel "for ever and ever and ever." The original Jack makes no such comment, and seems, at this juncture, a less likely candidate for lunacy than his adaptive double. As King himself has charged, the film paints Jack with a broader brush, leaving no doubt of where villainy lies (*Playboy* Interview 24).

The extent of Kubrick's omissions from this portion of the original text is sweeping; a fair comparison might be found in the hypothetical construction of a second Overlook, but with this version to be missing one entire wing. (Yet who could be certain that the hotel would not run more efficiently without that wing?) Even the most austere synopsis of "The Wasps' Nest" must include the following highlights: Working on the roof, Jack relives his clash with George Hatfield, a stutterer whom he dropped from the debate team at Stovington; the nastiness between the two led to Jack's termination (*Shining* 110–15). He presents Danny with a supposedly safe wasps' nest that turns out not to be safe after all; the dead wasps apparently regenerate and set upon the Torrances in the middle of the night (120–36). In the basement, Jack happens on a white leather scrapbook that captures much of the Overlook's unsavory history and inspires him to contemplate writing a book framing the hotel as an "index of the whole post–World War II American character" (152–87). For reasons even he does not understand, he calls Ullman and castigates him for not having disclosed the hotel's complete story (177–82). Jack's friend Al Shockley now calls Jack and flays him for bothering Ullman and for planning to write an exposé (186–90). Some time after, as Jack broods in the playground, the hedge animals begin skulking toward him, an experience that causes him to doubt his sanity (207–9). None of this material, which delineates the pressures, dreams, and torments weighing on Jack, appears in the film. So while Kubrick has us observe Jack's metamorphosis from troubled family man to deranged killer, he affords us only the most superficial explanation for it: the evil aura of the hotel, an aura that seems highly selective in whom it contaminates. From the opposite perspective, one recognizes that "The Wasps' Nest" contains some of King's clumsiest, flattest, most expendable writing; the narrative, lauded for its speed by Barbara Conaty (404) and Richard Lingeman (35), actually lumbers to a full, frustrating stop as Jack dawdles through the scrapbook (*Shining* 152–65). Kubrick's alterations guide the story away from clarity—which is not one of his objectives anyway—and toward a streamlined, if sometimes penumbral, simplicity.

The Crisis Realized

Kneeling in a hallway by himself, playing with his toy cars and trucks, Danny is intrigued when a tennis ball comes rolling up to him. He stands and ventures uneasily down the hall to Room 237, whose door is ajar. "Mom," he calls, "are you in there?" and then goes inside. Meanwhile Wendy, checking gauges in the boiler room, hears Jack groaning and screaming as if in agony. She runs to his aid and finds him asleep at his table, in the clutch of a nightmare. When she wakes him, he is extremely distraught; he dreamed that he killed her and Danny: cut them up "in little pieces." As she offers what comfort she can to him, Danny comes trudging toward them, thumb in his mouth. She bids her son go play in his room, but he does not seem to hear, and continues to advance like a sleepwalker. Scurrying to Danny, she is appalled to see that his neck is bruised. She turns ferociously on her husband: "You did this," she accuses. Jack, still stunned from his nightmare, shakes his head in denial, and, after she has exited with Danny, replies softly: "No."

This sequence departs from the original in two key respects, both of which undercut Jack's character in the film. The novel takes us, at least for a moment, into the room with Danny. Poking around, he discovers in the bathtub a hideous dead woman, "bloated and purple, her gas-filled belly rising out of the cold, ice-rimmed water like some fleshy island" (*Shining* 217). Suddenly, she sits up. Danny scrambles for the door, but is unable to open it, and the "years-damp, bloated, fish-smelling hands [close] softly around his throat and he [is] turned implacably around to stare into that dead and purple face" (218). In the novel, then, Danny's assailant is plainly identified—and it is not Jack. But whatever happens to the film Danny happens off-screen. Because we do not see the woman (or Danny or Jack, for that matter), we cannot rule out the possibility that Jack has tried to strangle his son. A second difference resides in the nature of Jack's dream. In the novel, his abusive father, seeming to speak over the radio, exhorts him to kill Danny and Wendy because a "real artist must suffer. Because each man kills the thing he loves. Because they'll always be conspiring against you ..." (227). Jack resists the exhortation, and, in his sleep, smashes the radio (228). By contrast, if the film Jack is urged on by his father, we are not made aware of it, and the dream-murders are in fact carried out; they are a *fait accompli*. Though each version of Jack is blameworthy, the film solicits our presumption of guilt more urgently than does the novel.

Mumbling to himself and gesticulating in anger, Jack wanders down the hall to the Gold Room. He flips on the lights, crosses to the bar, seats himself, and declares: "God, I'd give anything for a drink. I'd give my goddam soul for just a glass of beer." As if conjured by these words, a bartender named Lloyd materializes behind the (now stocked) bar, and, evincing a cordial familiarity with Jack, fills his request for bourbon. Lloyd is unfazed by his customer's shortage of money, and assures Jack that his credit is good. Between swallows, Jack announces that he is having a problem with the "old sperm bank upstairs." Specifically, he refutes Wendy's charge that he has injured Danny's neck—though once, he admits, he did hurt his son by pulling violently on his arm; that occurrence, in his view, was an accident. Carrying a baseball bat, a frantic Wendy now bursts into the room, rouses Jack from his reverie, and informs him that it was some "crazy woman in one of the rooms" who assaulted Danny. Jack, seeming drunk (though Lloyd and the liquor are no longer seen), asks: "Which room was it?"

Taken from Chapters 28 and 29, which total about 15 pages, the scene in the Gold Room is essentially a stellar example of adaptive reduction. The first several exchanges between Jack and Lloyd adhere closely to the novel, though we note that the fictional Lloyd's remarks are expressed as indirect quotations, suggestive of his insubstantiality:

> "Hi, Lloyd," [Jack says]. "A little slow tonight, isn't it?"
> Lloyd [says] that it [is]. Lloyd [asks] him what [will] it be.
> "Now I'm really glad you asked me that," Jack [says]....
> "Because I happen to have two tens and two twenties in my wallet, and I was afraid they'd be sitting there until sometime next April" [*Shining* 238–39].

But soon the fictional Jack's conversation veers off on a bitter, and remarkably wooden, tangent about life "on the wagon": how, from the gutter, this wagon seems the "biggest and best float in the whole parade," and yet how, from on board, it seems a kind of prison on wheels (240–41). When Wendy arrives, she has Danny with her. She and Jack begin quarreling, whereupon Danny stiffens and screams: "*Oh Daddy Daddy, it was her!*" (243). The "her" to whom Danny adverts is the horrid woman in the room, not Wendy, but his meaning is not established for several pages more. Indeed, the section immediately following the bar scene, Chapter 29, functions as an early denouement, in which Danny unfolds to his parents much of what he knows, and how he has come to know it—through shining. Only after a prolonged, laborious discussion does Jack resolve to visit the room and investigate (250). In remodeling this segment of the original, Kubrick has trimmed it skillfully, keeping what counts, and dropping the many time-consuming superfluities.

For a short stint, the film becomes less linear in its narration. The screen fills with the images and sounds of a local news program based in Miami. As anchor Glenn Rinker describes the prodigious snowstorm battering Colorado, we soon realize that we have been transported to Dick Hallorann's bedroom in Florida. A painting of a half-nude black woman adorns the wall over the television, and a similar portrait hangs on the wall behind the bed from which Dick impassively watches the news. Gradually the thudding of a heartbeat obtrudes, rising steadily in volume, and Dick's stony features take on a new aspect: his eyes widen and lift to the ceiling; his mouth opens; and he trembles as if in fear or astonishment. From the hallway in the Overlook, we see Room 237's open door, and now Danny is huddled someplace, shaking and drooling, his eyes glazed. As the heartbeat sound continues, we move inside 237. A hand—Jack's—slowly pushes open the door on an opulent bathroom. He gapes with terror, then lust, as a beautiful young woman, nude, pulls back the sheer white shower curtain, stands, and steps out of the tub. In dreamy slow-motion, they meet in the center of the bathroom, embrace, and kiss ardently. Sensing that something is wrong, Jack looks to a mirror, and sees that the woman in his arms has become a diseased old crone. She cackles loudly, and, as Danny continues in his trance, we see her lying supine in a bathtub, then shuffling toward the backpedaling Jack, then lifting herself to a sitting position in the tub. Moaning with fright, Jack dashes into the hall, locks the door, and backs away.

In the novel, the foregoing events are depicted separately and distinctly. But by designing this link in the narrative as something of a psychedelic montage, Kubrick accomplishes several ends at once. First, he imparts information integral to the story. We learn that Danny has made telepathic contact with Dick. We witness what Jack goes through in the room. We also receive an impression of what Danny encountered earlier—a dead woman in the tub, floating, then sitting up—though the fragments pertaining to Danny, severed from the novel, are apt to perplex. Second, Kubrick approximates the warped, tingling, unearthly feeling one imagines might mark a profound psychic episode, especially a terrifying one: enlightenment may be had, and will be, but only on harrowing terms. Finally, he achieves compaction, as a succession of events is combined into one powerful, and relatively short, experience.

The reintroduction of Dick to the film may be seen as both a contraction and an expansion of the source material. In the novel, Danny's first mental scream to his friend for help is emitted at the end of Part Four, "Snowbound," and is registered by Dick at the start of Part Five, "Matters of Life and Death" (*Shining* 306–12). The relevant pages permit us a fairly detailed glimpse of Dick's life in Florida. He jokes with Frank Masterton, the owner of the One-A Wholesale Vegetable Mart (309); meditates on dying—he has recently executed his will (310–11); and listens to Al Green on the radio while driving on State Highway 219 (310–11). In the film, he lies motionless in his bed: nothing more. Yet the message Dick receives seems to have become fuller and more complex across the narratives. In the novel, the dispatch is verbal: "*!!! OH DICK OH PLEASE PLEASE PLEASE COME!!!*" (306). While the content of the film message is somewhat ambiguous, it appears, from the way the narrative is constructed, that he is sent a stream of images beginning with Jack's entry into Room 237: Dick stares aghast at the ceiling, and then we move inside the haunted room. This interpretation is buttressed by the thunderous heartbeat that remains a constant over the shifting locations; it ties Dick to the happenings in 237, and argues that he is partaking of them. Transtextually, therefore, the verbal has become visual—and more layered.

What Jack confronts in the room is altogether different on the screen from on the page. The fictional Jack finds nothing unusual at first, even in the bathroom—the tub is "dry and empty" (*Shining* 252). But then he notices a bath mat on the floor—it should be in the linen cupboard—and smells a light, perfumed soap in the air (253). Preparing to leave, he hears a rattling, metallic noise in the bathroom, the sound of the shower curtain's being drawn back (253–54). From a distance, he thinks there may be someone or something in the tub, but then it may be just a "trick of the light" (254). Fearful, he steps into the hall and closes the door as, from inside, he seems to

> hear an odd wet thumping sound, far off, dim, as if something [has] just scrambled belatedly out of the tub, as if to greet a caller, as if it [has] realized the caller [is] leaving before the social amenities [have] been completed and so it [is] now rushing to the door, all purple and grinning, to invite the caller back inside. Perhaps forever [254].

Again, the film tilts to visuality, showing us something as opposed to nothing. That it shows us an attractive, young, nude woman who presently becomes decrepit and witchlike must give us pause. At the simplest level, Jack's desire for the seductress simply confirms his alienation from Wendy, and points to a sundering of the family. More deeply, the woman's transmogrification seems to speak of the sad turn Jack's life has taken (Davies, Farrell, and Matthews 340): his marriage, his writing, his sanity, and his self-worth, once intact, have all disintegrated. Through visual symbols, the film projects the ruinous and frightful path that Jack is traveling.

His brow knit, Dick tries to call the Overlook but cannot get through. At the hotel, Jack reports to Wendy that he explored the room and saw nothing out of the ordinary, "not one goddam thing." Although she does not challenge his word, she clearly finds his statement difficult to accept. What, she asks, is his explanation for the bruises on Danny's neck? Jack answers that Danny must have injured himself, which, he contends, is not implausible in light of the spell the boy suffered before their move to the Overlook. In bed, Danny is deep into another trance: he hears their discussion, sees "REDRUM" scrawled on a door, and watches another deluge of blood slosh out of the elevator. Wendy proposes that they must get Danny out of the hotel, causing Jack's temper to flare. He objects heatedly that he is progressing in his work, and would have no credible opportunities back in Boulder. He then storms out of their apartment as Wendy dissolves into tears.

The film's handling of these incidents varies only slightly from the novel's. In small ways, Kubrick tightens the pace of the narrative, avoiding needless delays. Originally, for example, before arguing that Danny's bruises are self-inflicted, Jack hypothesizes that they could be stigmata, and launches into a tortuous speech on the interaction between the mind and the body (*Shining* 265). The passage is a narrational loop-the-loop that adds little to the story but time. Similarly, when the fictional Wendy submits that they must get Danny away from the hotel, Jack seems resistant, but does agree to attempt an evacuation by snowmobile (263–64). Eventually, of course, he reneges on his agreement, and disables the snowmobile by removing its magneto, which he flings into a field of snow (282). Such temporizing is unneeded and unmissed by the film. On a different front, Kubrick waits until this late stage to invoke the mantra "REDRUM," which appears as early as page 32 in the novel, and sporadically thereafter. By keeping the word cloaked until now, Kubrick invests it with grander importance—it becomes climactic, and not just one vision of many. We understand that the narrative has been elevated one notch closer to its summit.

As Dick continues trying to glean information about the situation at the Overlook, Jack rages through some rear enclave of the kitchen. He emerges into a hallway and pauses, seeing festive ribbons and balloons on the floor, and hearing 1920s music echoing faintly off the walls. His anger forgotten, he saunters into the Gold Room, the source of the music, and proceeds to the bar, unperturbed by the milling crowd of people around him. He is greeted by Lloyd, who pours him a bourbon on the rocks, free of charge. Jack wants to know who is allowing him to drink gratis, but when Lloyd declines to tell, Jack smiles, shrugs, and ambles away. Seconds later, he collides with a waiter, who accidentally spatters him with avocado dip; the two men repair to the restroom to tidy Jack up. Setting to work on him, the man identifies himself as Delbert Grady, a name that prompts a string of nervous but accusatory questions from Jack. Grady unctuously denies that he was ever the caretaker at the Overlook, that he murdered his wife and daughters, and that he killed himself. Becoming assertive, he maintains that Jack is the caretaker, and always has been. He advises Jack that Danny, through mysterious means, is endeavoring to bring in an "outside party"–Dick Hallorann. Jack labels Danny a "willful boy," and Grady concurs, suggesting that Jack's son and wife should both be "corrected." Apparently reversing his earlier statement, Grady admits having "corrected" his own wife and children.

In reaching this plateau, the film has omitted sizable chunks of the original narrative. Soon after his first visit to Room 217, the fictional Jack goes there a second time, in a vivid dream. He enters the bathroom, flings back the shower curtain, and finds lying in the tub his old nemesis George Hatfield, naked, with a knife rammed into his chest. Hatfield climbs out of the tub, and, still vengeful at being dropped from the debate team, tries to strangle Jack (*Shining* 271). Later, in accordance with omens King has duly sprinkled beforehand, Danny is mauled by a pride of snow-powdered hedge lions (289–91). Though the attack draws blood, the real injury comes when his father claims not to believe him, and slaps his face (294). Still later, Jack, distracted by his research, realizes that he has not emptied the boiler lately, meaning that it—and the Overlook—are on the verge of exploding. After some deliberation, he spins the valve and relieves the pressure; his second trip to the Gold Room is spurred by his conviction that the hotel will reward him with a drink for having saved it (326–31). All these omissions relate to strands of the original plot that Kubrick judged, from the outset, dispensable: the Stovington days, the unwieldy hedge animals. (Even the elimination of the boiler incident evolves from Kubrick's distaste for the enchanted hedges, which he replaces with the maze. Since it makes thematic sense for the film Jack to perish in the maze, as he finally does, it would be illogical to draw the viewers' attention to the boiler, which plays no part in his demise.) Once more, Kubrick opts for speed over depth.

The sequence in the Gold Room to which the film leaps is rooted in Chapters 43 and 44 of the novel. Much of the fictional Jack's conversation with the satanic Lloyd (we cannot fail to notice the bright red lapels of his jacket, shaped like horns) arrives onscreen virtually undisturbed:

> "Hello, boys," Jack Torrance [says] softly. "I've been away but now I'm back."
> "Good evening, Mr. Torrance," Lloyd [says], genuinely pleased. "It's good to see you."
> ....
> "No charge to you, Mr. Torrance.... Your money is no good here. Orders from the manager" [*Shining* 341–42].

But in the novel, Lloyd and the other specters use this moment to indicate their strong interest in acquiring Danny, whom they see as a "talented boy" (342). It is an interest that troubles Jack acutely, and to which he accedes only with reluctance, and only under duress (342–44). Unlike the film Jack, the original version still feels some remnant of caring for his family; his villainy, though ample, is not now pure, and indeed never is.

Jack's intense dialog with Grady drew a hostile assessment from critics, who deemed it flawed on various grounds. Pauline Kael wrote that the scene brings the film to a "dead halt, from which it never fully recovers" ("Devolution" 139); she also regretted Grady's reference to Dick as a "nigger cook." So vicious are the demons in this film, she tweaked, that they are even racists (144). Though the first complaint has less legitimacy than the second, it should be noted that both the static quality of the conversation and Grady's slur originate in the novel (*Shining* 348–51). Richard Jameson derided the scene for its conspicuous want of logic. Grady, he observed, assures Jack that Jack has never seen him before, that Grady himself has no memory of ever having been the caretaker, that Jack has always been the caretaker, and that Grady was obliged to discipline his family when they interfered with his caretaking (31–32). Jameson's criticisms are not unjust, but again, one appreciates that Grady's collapsible argument is derived faithfully from the novel (*Shining* 348–49). In fact, the film exchange differs from the original in only two salient ways. Kubrick takes the men from the bar to the red-accented restroom, isolating Jack and lending the moment a more crystalline focus, and he suppresses any appeal by Grady to Jack's ambition (351). In the film, Jack has no ambition to which Grady might appeal.

Talking to herself, Wendy paces back and forth planning how

she and Danny–and perhaps Jack–can escape the hotel. She is distressed to hear shouts of "REDRUM" coming from her son's bedroom. When she goes to his side, she is told by Tony that Danny's personality has "gone away," having been eclipsed by that of his alter ego. In another part of the hotel, Jack neatly disables the CB radio. Dick now learns that the Forest Service has been unable to raise the Torrances, and, by morning, he is on a plane bound for Denver. From the airport, he calls Larry Durkin of Durkin's Garage to arrange for a Sno-Cat that he can take to the Overlook. Challenging the hazardous weather, he rents a car and begins his journey to Durkin's, as Wendy and Danny stare vapidly at their television. (As before, the fare is *Roadrunner* cartoons.) She informs Danny, who is still literally not himself, that she must leave to speak with Jack but will return soon; she arms herself with a baseball bat.

The film's departures from its source through this stretch are few but telling. In the novel, Danny's personality remains his own, and Tony—a helpful agent anyway—now comes only rarely: the forces in the hotel have conspired to keep him at a distance (*Shining* 323). Even so, the fictional Danny is a wellspring of knowledge and comfort to his frazzled mother, updating her on Jack's movements, on the call to Dick, and on the situation generally (323–24). In giving us a Danny who is disturbed and debilitated, the film exacerbates the crisis, pushing the drama toward melodrama: the plight of mother and son seems hopeless. As to Jack, in the original text he destroys the radio while asleep (227–28); it is hardly an act for which he could be held responsible. But the film Jack, though muzzy, is wide-awake when he exposes the radio's inner workings and removes three vital components—his behavior is wanton, calculated, and unmistakably villainous. For his part, the fictional Dick must surmount a rash of difficulties before he can leave Florida: he must lie to his boss, a Mr. Queems, to get three days off; he must weather additional telepathic screams from Danny so piercing that they hurt him physically; and he must accept a speeding ticket from a sarcastic police officer (314–21). From our perspective, the film Dick simply appears on his plane.

Gripping her bat, Wendy ventures into the Colorado Lounge searching for Jack, who is not to be seen. She goes to his worktable,

Alert and helpful in the novel, Danny becomes distracted in the film, exacerbating Wendy's plight.

and, as curiosity shades into dismay and horror, she scans through the material he has typed. Every sheet, and there are hundreds of them, has been filled with the same sentence repeated ad infinitum: "All work and no play makes Jack a dull boy." Jack now emerges from behind a wall, startling her; his mood is eerie, at once lighthearted and sinister. Though she has obviously lost her will to communicate with him, he compels her to, proposing that Danny (who tunes them in from afar) has been weighing on her mind. She admits, through her sobs, that she believes Danny should be taken to a doctor. Jack, totally unsympathetic, mocks her, backing her toward the staircase. His anger rising to the surface, he accuses her of self-centeredness, of being blind to his moral and contractual commitments to the Overlook. He slowly pursues her up the stairs, and she begins to chop at him with the bat. Soon after he promises to bash in her brains, she strikes his hand, then clubs him over the head, sending him tumbling down the steps to lie unconscious on his face. Now she drags him to the storage room, and, as he comes to, imprisons

If Jack's morality is ambiguous in the source, the film portrays him as wholly villainous.

him. From behind the locked door, Jack desperately employs an assortment of rhetorical tactics: he blusters at her, reasons with her, appeals to her pity—all to no avail. When she tells him she plans to take Danny by Sno-Cat to Sidewinder, he becomes amused, and suggests she investigate the vehicle. She does, and discovers that it, like the radio, has been sabotaged.

This leg of the narrative is bolder and splashier in the film than in the novel. Wendy's devastating discovery that Jack's literary project consists of the same insipid sentence typed over and over does not occur in the book. But the effect of the film's point-of-view shot is shattering, as Wendy's hand flails through the stack of paper, and each sheet is found to be a permutation of the one before. The moment is epiphanic—Jack, the pages tell us, is truly insane, and this truth is conveyed not verbally (since the typed sentence itself says nothing) but visually. Though the fictional Jack mocks Wendy a bit—"Jack, I want to help," she says; "Oh yeah," he replies: "You and Danny only want to *help*" (*Shining* 367)—this tendency is magnified in the film. To be sure, the film Jack's oddly mixed tone, complemented by his wild facial expressions, is more frightening than pure wrath, and the text will continue to tap Jack Nicholson's talents in this regard. In the novel, Jack and Wendy do battle in the Colorado Lounge; he tries to strangle her, and she cracks him over the head with a straw-wrapped wine bottle. Reacting, he rocks back on his heels, loosens his grip, and falls to the floor (366–69). How much more visually exciting, in the film, is Jack's rolling, bouncing flight down the stairs. Finally, in the novel, Wendy is assisted by Danny, who even helps her drag Jack to his pantry-prison (372–73). But the film Wendy enjoys no such support, and must depend on her own resources; we are encouraged to acknowledge this young woman's growth from vacillating timidity to self-reliant action. In greater measure than the book, the film here makes a feminist statement.

Climax and Resolution

After a short lull, the pitch of the film again escalates. Still trapped in the storage room, Jack is roused from his sleep by a knock on the door. His visitor, who remains outside, and whose voice is now strangely reboant, is Grady. Grady ridicules Jack over the sorry state to which he has come, and doubts openly that Jack is capable of dealing properly with his family. When Jack gives his word that he will meet Grady's harsh standard, the ghost sets him free. Meanwhile Dick, in a Sno-Cat, rolls on toward the Overlook. As Wendy sleeps in bed, Danny, bleating the word "REDRUM," picks up the outsized knife she keeps on the nightstand; for a moment it appears he may attack her. Then he turns and goes to the dresser, finds a tube of lipstick, and uses it to write "REDRUM" on the bedroom door. Suddenly, as he studies his handiwork, his mutterings become raspy shouts that waken his mother; the mirror reflects the word on the door back to her as "MURDER."

The film's representations of Jack and Dick do not differ widely from those in the novel, although the characters have become simplified in transition. In the case of the fictional Jack, he is awake when we join him, nibbling at Triscuits and ruminating bitterly on how his life has crumbled. We, of course, are privy to his rambling thoughts: to his resentment of Wendy and Danny, his recollection of a Frank Norris novel, his nourishment of a new respect for his own martinet of a father (*Shining* 378-80). Jack's musings do not benefit the story particularly—they are filler—and could not have been brought gracefully to the screen in any event. His conversation with Grady is longer in the novel than in the film (381—82), but each is the substantial equivalent of the other. The texture surrounding Dick is likewise reduced to a minimum for the film, much as happens with his stay in Florida. In the novel, we witness his procuring of the snowmobile from Durkin, who trades him coats and gives him a ski mask (400-2). We are also subjected to Dick's tussle with a hedge lion that causes him to wreck, claws him, but then scampers away when Dick sets it aflame (405-13). While this last piece of business was excluded for reasons of compatibility, the end result of all these omissions is increased narrative speed.

Conversely, the interaction between Wendy and Danny does show some secondary inventiveness. As indicated, the fictional Danny stays clearheaded; he never does brandish a knife over his sleeping mother. By having him do so in the film, Kubrick seeks to produce a frisson in the viewer—perhaps cheaply, since Danny's having the knife serves no utilitarian purpose other than scaring us. His printing "REDRUM" on the door is a variation of a development at the end of the novel's Part Four. Examining an obscene clock in the ballroom, Danny has a vision in which he sees "REDRUM" flashing off and on in his parents' medicine cabinet mirror.

> [A] huge clock in a glass bowl materialize[s] in front of it. There [are] no hands or numbers on the clockface, only a date written in red: DECEMBER 2. And then, eyes widening in horror, he [sees] the word REDRUM reflecting dimly from the glass dome, now reflected twice. And he [sees] that it spell[s] MURDER [306].

In its turn, the film involves Wendy in the revelation, as arguably she should be: Jack is coming primarily for her. And certainly the film's timing is more dramatic than the novel's; no sooner is the word demystified for her (and for us) than Jack fiercely announces his presence.

Using a long-handled ax, he begins breaking his way into the apartment, destroying the door. Wendy and Danny retreat to the bathroom, where she lifts Danny through a window; he slides down a snowbank to temporary safety. She tries to take the same route, but cannot fit through any of the small, ice-jammed windows, and Jack, alluding to the fable of the three little pigs, starts tearing through the bathroom door. As he is about to gain entry, she hacks his hand with her knife, and Dick arrives at the hotel—Jack and Wendy both hear the rumbling of the Sno-Cat. Back inside, Danny hides in a metallic storage bin. Jack now interrupts his attack on Wendy to go limping in the direction of Dick, whose reconnoitering of the hotel is somewhat incautious. "Hello," he calls. "Anybody here?" Jack springs from behind a pillar, and, bellowing, kills Dick with a single ax-blow to the chest. The murder brings a sympathetic scream from Danny, which Jack hears. He sets out after his son, who abandons his hiding place and darts down a hall. Jack, carrying his bloodstained ax, hobbles after him.

Though Kubrick here retains the overall shape of the original narrative, he imposes several new wrinkles on it. The fictional Jack's weapon is a roque mallet (*Shining* 382–429); it is a blunt, crude instrument, and potentially lethal, but just not as impressive visually as an ax. The ax is more thrilling. Yet the fictional Jack does considerable damage with what he has, and especially to Wendy. Having surprised her at the foot of the stairs, he swings the mallet at her, missing but causing her to stumble, then slams its head into her stomach. She "scream[s], suddenly submerged in an ocean of pain" (396). Moments later, he hammers her "just below the line of her breasts, breaking two ribs. She [falls] forward on the steps and new agony [rips] her …" (397). The film Jack is no less murderous in his intentions, but never makes physical contact with his wife. His relative inefficiency permits us to feel frightened and giddy without feeling outraged and indignant. If, in the novel, Jack calls Wendy a "pig" (410), he elaborates this epithet, in the film, into tragicomic verse: "'Little pigs, little pigs, let me come in.' 'Not by the hair on your chinny-chin-chin.' 'Then I'll huff and I'll puff and I'll blow your house in.'" The allusion also recalls a threat made to Danny by a ghostly "dogman" in the main corridor (333–34), and gives acknowledgment, in an outlandish setting, of King's liberal co-option of fairy tales and children's fantasies (Curran 33–46). Doubtless Kubrick's most striking innovation is the murder of Dick, who, in the novel, has his cheekbone shattered by Jack's mallet (*Shining* 416), but who does survive. One might wonder why, rhetorically, a modestly heroic character—a man gifted with clairvoyance, which ought to warn him—would be imported from across the country in a rescue attempt, only to die preemptively in an ambush. Possible answers include: his death generates horror; it confirms the peril that Wendy and Danny are in; and his presence supplies the Sno-Cat whereby Wendy and Danny escape. Pauline Kael has her own speculation, which should not necessarily be discounted: "The awful suspicion pops into the mind that since we don't want to see Wendy or Danny hurt and there's nobody else alive around for Jack to get at, he's given the black man" ("Devolution" 144).

Ascending a flight of stairs, Wendy hears chanting, indistinct voices, and presently sees an extraordinary sight: in a bedroom, someone wearing a dog costume is evidently performing a sexual act on a man who is formally dressed. The participants stop and stare at her. Jack now follows Danny outside and into the gray-white maze, and the film begins to oscillate between activities in the maze and those in the hotel. Rushing through the Overlook, Wendy discovers the gory body of Dick, and is met by a man who, blood streaming down his face, raises a glass to her and smiles: "Great party, isn't it?" As Jack continues to chase his son, Wendy plunges into a room that is inexplicably hung with cobwebs and filled with skeletons. In the maze, Danny ingeniously backtracks over some of his footprints, leaps off to the side, and ensconces himself in the hedges. Quivering with fear, Wendy is tormented by a vision familiar to Danny: blood cascades from the elevator and washes toward her. Jack, faltering in the cold, is fooled by Danny's stratagem, and soon becomes disoriented while Danny slips around him and heads back to the exit. Crying "Mommy! Mommy!" the boy shoots out of the maze and into his mother's waiting arms.

This turbulent sequence mixes together some of King's ideas and some of Kubrick's. The shot of the decadent couple in the bedroom has its origin in Chapter 44, at which point Jack, dancing at

The film is generally less violent than the book. Whereas the original Wendy stabs her husband in the back, the adaptive version merely cuts his hand.

the bustling bar, is about to have his first encounter with Grady. Among the revelers are Harry Derwent, a onetime owner of the Overlook, and a man named Roger, who is cavorting in a dog costume (and who has earlier, we infer, harassed Danny) (*Shining* 346–47). Harry is described as "AC/DC," while Roger is "only DC. He spent a weekend with Harry in Cuba once ..." (347). Their fleeting appearance in the film adds a kinky new dimension to the hotel's already unwholesome atmosphere. Though Wendy does not actually see the couple in the novel, she *is* accosted by a man in a green ghoul-mask who blurts: "*Great party, isn't it?*" (406), and she does find Dick on the floor, bloody but still breathing (425). The film strikes off on its own, however, when it omits a final, moving exchange between Jack and Danny. Cornered by his possessed father, Danny offers: "Go on and hit me" (428). The real Jack, the human Jack, reasserts himself long enough to tell "Doc": "Run away. Quick. And remember how much I love you" (428). No such wavering is seen in the film Jack, whose purpose is constant. Having snubbed that sentimental opportunity, the film seizes on another: emerging from the maze, Danny repeatedly addresses his mother as "Mommy" and not, as Tony would have, "Mrs. Torrance." Wendy, the film lets us know, has recovered her son, and a glimmer of happiness has sneaked into the conclusion.

Wendy and Danny climb into Dick's Sno-Cat and drive away as Jack, roaring mindlessly, staggers around inside the maze and at last collapses. Without warning, the film bounds ahead to show us a shot of Jack in daylight, seated dead in the maze, his face rimed with ice, his eyes and mouth frozen open. As the 1920s theme music rises, we cut back inside the Overlook, and track into the Gold Room. Smoothly we draw closer and closer to a rectangular arrangement of 21 black-and-white photographs on the wall. Zeroing in on the one in the center, we see a throng of smartly dressed men and women, pressed together in a capacious room, responding gaily to the camera. Their hairstyles, clothing, and accouterments are of the 1920s. Centered and foregrounded stands a younger-looking Jack Torrance, smiling and waving. Beneath his image is the inscription: "Overlook Hotel / July 4th Ball / 1921." The closing credits ensue.

Two familial texts could scarcely end in less like-minded ways. In the novel, Jack, or what is left of him—he is referred to now as a "thing," as "it" (*Shining* 426), or as the "manager/caretaker" (433)—dies when the boiler explodes and the hotel is consumed by a fire (433–41). Dick goes on to find work at the Red Arrow Lodge in Maine (442), and Wendy accepts the offer of a job in Maryland from Al Shockley (443–44). Insofar as the virtuous characters are mending, and Jack is dead, the conclusion exudes poetic justice. One might also note that its rhetoric, which delivers clarification and closure, is both conventional and intelligible. In the film, though we have hopes that the remaining Torrances may yet prosper, Dick is dead, and poetic justice is maimed. Moreover, the text's final rhetorical gambit, the picture of Jack from 1921, is neither conventional nor supremely intelligible. What does it mean? Two of Jack's comments would seem to contain clues to the riddle. Early on, he mentions his feeling of déjà vu in coming to the Overlook; so perhaps, somehow, Jack has indeed been here before. He also voices his desire to remain at the hotel forever; so perhaps, somehow, he will. But how or why these improbabilities should be, and what we are to make of them, are left murky. The film's ending, which Henry Bromell classified as "crisp" but "confusing" (83), raises more questions than it settles.

While such an abstraction is rather difficult to measure, Kubrick's *The Shining* seems not so faithful an adaptation as his *Lolita*. In translating King's novel, the director has excluded large segments of the original plot, and revamped other segments severely to suit his own needs and sensibilities. Alexander Pope submitted that no artwork is "faultless" (lines 253–54), and this film does not disprove his maxim. With its spotty logic, bas-relief characterizations, and baffling references and theme, the film is faulty. Yet it is no more so than the inflated, repetitious, prosaic novel on which it is based. In fact, the film often rises to heights that the source never attains, and its rhetoric, though sometimes inscrutable, is, unlike the original's, always energetic. If King's novel is fuller, rounder, and easier to follow than Kubrick's film, it is also less exhilarating. The adaptive text has, to paraphrase Shakespeare's Gertrude, less matter but more art.

Chapter 4
Full Metal Jacket

Full Metal Jacket was adapted from a 1979 novel by Gustav Hasford, his first, entitled *The Short-Timers*; he has since published *The Phantom Blooper* and *A Gypsy Good Time*. An unabatedly morbid work, *The Short-Timers* follows a young man known as "Joker" from Marine Corps basic training at Parris Island to combat in Vietnam, where he becomes a full-fledged "minister of death" (Hasford 4). The book's opening section concerns Joker's ambivalent relationship with a hapless recruit nicknamed "Pyle," and Pyle's own troubled relationship with the other recruits and with their brutal drill instructor, Sergeant Gerheim. Eventually Pyle develops superior skills, but at the cost of his sanity: on graduation day, he kills his sergeant and then himself. The novel abruptly flashes ahead to the Vietnam War, in which Joker finds himself a combat correspondent.

At Hue, he falls in with the misfits of the self-proclaimed Lusthog Squad, and participates in atrocity-marred fighting. After one engagement, he dispatches a wounded, teenage, female sniper by shooting her through the head. Later, he and his fellow Marines face another sniper, this one in the jungle at Khe Sanh. Laughing, the sniper slowly decimates the squad, and Joker performs a mercy killing on his friend Cowboy, who has been grievously wounded. Now in command, Joker turns the survivors around and moves them back down the trail, the mission aborted.

Hasford's novel aspires to burn with what Walter Pater famously called a hard, gemlike flame: it is taut, slangy, epigrammatic, and completely unsentimental. At 180 pages in paperback and perhaps

50,000 words, it is also quite spare, and reads as much like a Hollywood "treatment" as like a bona fide novel (Straczynski 159–61). Most critics lauded *The Short-Timers*. *The Virginia Quarterly Review* termed Hasford's style "direct and shocking" (100), and *Kirkus Reviews* saw a "terse spitball of a book, fine and real and terrifying, that marks a real advance in Vietnam war literature" (1209). Francis Curtis praised its disturbing realism (77), while Walter Clemons declared it "extremely ugly," but the "best work of fiction about the Vietnam War" that he had read (60). Offering dissent, Roger Sale decried the novel for prose that seems to reek of "Creative Writing 201," and for its absence of a cogent point of view: "Everything just happens" (19). Jack Beatty found Hasford's obsession with death a "bore," the product of a meager imagination (40). More than one critic, incidentally, detected the influence of Joseph Heller's satirical masterpiece *Catch-22* (Clemons 60; Sale 19).

Explaining what attracted him to *The Short-Timers*, Kubrick himself extolled its "compelling story" (Lacayo 11). But what, one might inquire, did he see in the story that made it seem so compelling? In violation of his stated criterion, the novel focuses more on the outer than on the inner life of its characters (Kubrick 306); it is a work presided over by action and dialog, not by introspection and contained emotion. Since Joker is the first-person narrator, we do have some access to his mentation—but his internal world is depressingly barren, and manifests itself mainly in wisecracks, cynicisms, and cant. Yet one must recognize that Hasford's novel does have its enticements. A war story, it is overflowing with opportunities to manipulate "flesh and feeling" as Kubrick desires (308); dealing acridly with America's longest and most frustrating conflict, it crackles with something like a "passionate sense of truth" (Reynolds 144). It is also shot through with surrealism, another quality that the director appreciates (Houston 44): we lurch into characters named General Motors and Chili Vendor, a character who kisses a dead rat (Hasford 70), and still another who eats human flesh (74). As Richard Lacayo supposed, Kubrick

> didn't find a story, he found a Kubrick movie, and one that could be made without boiling off half the book, as he did with *The Shining*,

... to arrive at his perennial obsessions. [The] novel had arrived at those already: death and technological fetishism, of course, but above all scorn for the phantom of liberty, for the false presumption that we're masters of our fate [11].

Michael Herr, author of *Dispatches,* collaborated with Kubrick and Hasford on the screenplay for *Full Metal Jacket,* and later wrote about the experience. He reports that in the spring of 1980, Kubrick was casting around for a war story—and by "story" Kubrick meant a "book of such agreeable elements and proportions that he could break it down and build it up again as film; a tree with perfect branches" (Herr v). Having selected *The Short-Timers,* Kubrick conferred periodically with Herr for years, usually by telephone, about how an artist might put the "living, breathing presence" of what Jung dubbed the shadow, the darkest sliver of the unconscious, into a book or film (v). So fascinating were the conversations—Kubrick's store of information was "tremendous"—that Herr accepted them as their own reward (v). Taking his direction from the unique, "pre-cliché" dialog of the novel, Kubrick determined to fashion a film whose

> moral and political trellises are down, with all the rhetoric that grew on them. The audience would not be told how to watch this movie, nor which emotions they're supposed to be locating. This would be what the studios used to call a "Who Do You Root For?" movie, nonexplicit in its meanings, low-road in its production, minimal in expression; highly specific, like Hemingway. Simple surface, long reverberations [vi].

In a kind of round-robin, Herr, Hasford, and Kubrick took turns writing and rewriting the script, which Kubrick continued to polish "all through shooting" (vi).

Critical reactions to *Full Metal Jacket* tended to form around three epicenters. First, fixing on the film's bipartite structure, many critics viewed the work as two technically joined, but essentially separate, entities. From this perspective, the initial (Parris Island) segment was generally held in higher esteem than the concluding (Vietnam) segment (Corliss, "Welcome" 66; Denby 54; Kael, "Ponderoso" 75; Lacayo 14; Reaves 226). The remarks of Pauline Kael, in this connection, did not stand in isolation: "After the first part reaches climax, the movie becomes dispersed, as if it had no story. It never regains its forward drive; the second part is almost a different picture…" ("Ponderoso" 75). Second, a fair—and by now growing—number of critics chastised Kubrick for his apparent elevation of technique, and technology, over human values. He is "not interested in character…," Tom O'Brien claimed, "but [in] an idea" (458). "No one in his [or her] right mind could mistake Kubrick for a humanist," David Denby chimed in (54). John Simon charged that the film "lacks a human center" ("Bullet" 52), and Gerri Reaves, who was inclined to agree, nevertheless supplied Kubrick's imagined retort: "So does the world" (229). Third, and most pertinent to this study, several critics saw fit to comment on the relation of the film to its source, though one observer's comments seldom aligned precisely with anyone else's. Richard Corliss asserted that the director "closely followed" the novel up to the film's "Hollywood ending" ("Welcome" 66). Kael found that the original Joker, inflamed by a fierce revulsion at himself and his surroundings, does "horrible things" that the film Joker, restrained by Kubrick, does not ("Ponderoso" 76). Reaves noted that Kubrick broadens the narrational point of view, and, while preserving plenty of the novel's details, relocates some of them to create new effects (233). At least two critics faulted him for being too faithful to his source: O'Brien and Lacayo questioned his decision to kill off the Draconian sergeant (458; 14).

Like others, I recognize the film's dichotomous design. My analysis, in shaping itself to the film, is therefore similarly designed.

Parris Island

Exposition

The film begins with music. Even before the "Warner Bros." logo fades from view, we hear the mournful strains of a steel guitar, leading into Johnny Wright's country classic "Hello, Vietnam." The music continues through the opening credits—blocky white letters against a jet background that spell out "A STANLEY KUBRICK FILM" and then "FULL METAL JACKET"—and on through the inaugural series of shots. These shots present, in well-lit close-up, one young man after another getting his head shaved; most of the men appear dour and abstracted. A shot of the floor shows it to be forested with thick, curling chunks of hair. Not to be ignored are the song's lyrics, which run as follows:

> Kiss me good-bye and write me while I'm gone;
> Good-bye, my sweetheart; hello, Vietnam.
> America has heard the bugle call,
> And you know, it involves us one and all.
> I don't suppose that war will ever end;
> There's fighting that will break us up again.
> Good-bye, my darling; hello, Vietnam.
> Though here to take a battle to be won ...
> Kiss me good-bye and write me while I'm gone;
> Good-bye, my sweetheart; hello, Vietnam.

None of this material is evident in the novel, which begins with Gerheim's confronting the recruits. As with *Lolita* and *The Shining*, Kubrick has assembled a prolog that not only rivets our attention but presages the tone of the film—a tone, in this instance, that mingles violence, irony, and black humor. The titles we see are stark and uncompromising, hinting of extremes, yet the twangy, homespun music undercuts their somberness. We are instructed, in effect, that what is about to happen will be quite serious, but will be nuanced in such a way as to keep us off-balance. The song's heartfelt but simpleminded lyrics extend this message; our musical narrator refers to America's hearing a "bugle call" (in fact, some citizens heard it and some emphatically did not) and says "hello" to a place and an event that would destroy lives by the tens of thousands. A weird, rhetorical dissonance has begun to function. The head-shaving, of course, is something of a set piece in films that depict boot camp, but it still retains the power to appall, and especially when one remembers that the long hair of the late 1960s was not merely a bow to fashion but, very often, a symbol of political protest. As Terrence Rafferty realized, the recruits' heads are shaved "for surgery: basic training is an operation on their brains, a procedure that excises, with laserlike precision, all traces of humane and civilized impulses." (98). The men are not actually harmed in this sequence, but the possibility that they could be, by the Corps or by some other, is immediately thinkable.

Clad in green fatigues, they stand at rigid attention in front of their bunks as Gunnery Sergeant Hartman, their senior drill instructor, moves before them. His orientation speech, delivered on the prowl, is blistering. He addresses the men as "maggots," "ladies," and, most spectacularly, as "unorganized grabasstic [sic] pieces of amphibian shit." He advises them that he will be hard but fair, and that every recruit who completes the training session will be a "weapon, ... a minister of death, praying for war." Hartman now begins to single out recruits for particular abuse, branding them with belittling cognomens. He renames Private Brown, a black, Private "Snowball," after which, across the barracks, another recruit adopts John Wayne's voice to mutter impudently: "Is that you, John Wayne? Is this me?" The incident enrages Hartman, and when the culprit admits his guilt, the sergeant renames him Private "Joker," then crumples him with a fist to the midsection. Hartman next descends on a recruit whom he excoriates for his modest height and for hailing from the state of Texas; Hartman renames him Private "Cowboy." His next target is the rotund Leonard Lawrence, whom Hartman designates a "fatbody," and renames Private "Gomer Pyle." Hartman orders Pyle to cease smirking; when Pyle proves unable to, Hartman has him drop to his knees and place his throat on Hartman's clenching hand. The vicious stranglehold dispels the smirk, and Hartman warns Pyle that he had better "square [himself] away."

The film's Parris Island segment is drawn from the novel's first major division, entitled "The Spirit of the Bayonet," which is barely 30 pages long. One is therefore unsurprised to learn that the film not only changes the "Bayonet" section, but expands and enriches it—a procedure that a novel-based adaptation rarely undertakes. Sergeant Gerheim becomes Sergeant Hartman, whose surname, suggesting "heart of man" (Reaves 227), asks us to consider: Does the sergeant truly represent the quintessence of humanity, or is Kubrick being ironic? Hartman is not exactly a villain, but he is certainly an adversarial figure and the personification of Marine rigor and discipline. One observes, in this context, that his role is being enlarged and made even more colorful than in the original. If Gerheim first laughs at Joker's effrontery, then mildly dresses him down, (Hasford 4), Hartman and his rhetoric sky to dizzying heights of imaginative spleen. Swooping across the spotless floor, he demands:

> Who said that? Who the fuck said that? Who's the slimy little communist shit twinkle-toed cocksucker down here, who just signed his own death warrant? Nobody, huh? The fairy fucking godmother said it! Out-fucking-standing! I will P. T. you all until you fucking die! I'll P. T. you until your assholes are sucking buttermilk!

Magnificent, near-poetic invective, this speech and many more of its kind pump Hartman to proportions that are almost, but not quite, heroic. Yet the scene does not overlook the other principals—Joker, Cowboy, and Pyle—and accords them each a distinct, introductory moment; the novel, by contrast, glosses them over, especially Cowboy (3–7). Finally, the film here initiates two adaptive trends that will continue throughout the text: displacement of lines from one character or situation to another, and, remarkably, a decrease in the level of violence. The John Wayne line is switched from Cowboy (4) to the more important Joker. Gerheim does not choke Pyle but rather strikes him four times—once each in the Adam's apple, chest, stomach, and face (6).

As Joker's voice-over tells us where we are—Parris Island—and what the place is—a Marine college for the "phony-tough and the crazy-brave"—we see the recruits entering into their training. Calling cadence, Hartman double-times them down a quiet suburban street. We cut next to a practice field where, silhouetted against the orange sun, the men climb on ropes and ladders. A dissolve takes us to a parade deck, on which Hartman puts them through a series of marching maneuvers. When Pyle lowers his rifle to the wrong shoulder, Hartman reviles him and strikes him twice, knocking off his cap. After another dissolve, we watch the platoon marching along the parade deck; trailing the others, Pyle marches by himself, his pants around his ankles, his right thumb in his mouth, his cap on backwards, and his rifle held upside down.

This sequence adheres to the broad thrust of the novel, but differs in niceties. Joker's voice-over is a residuum from the first-person fictional narration; it indicates that the story is being told primarily, though not absolutely, from his vantage, and positions him as the pivotal character. (David Denby carefully resisted identifying Joker as the "protagonist," arguing that he is incapable of holding the film together [55].) The early training is mentioned in the source (Hasford 7), but goes undescribed. By showing us the recruits at labor, the film fleshes in the book's outline, gives us an idea of what the grueling life is like, and vivifies the narrative. A few pages into the novel, we are informed that Pyle is receiving "more than his share of the beatings" (7), but they occur off-page; they are not represented. Nor is Pyle subjected, at this preliminary stage, to any extraordinary humiliation. That we see Pyle's being pummeled speaks of the film's directness and visuality; his public ridicule on the parade deck is likewise visual, and suggests a slightly quickened pace, even as the narrative becomes fuller.

Strutting through the barracks, Hartman lets his charges know that tonight they will sleep with their rifles. Moreover, they will give their rifles feminine names; the men are effectively married to their weapons. The sergeant orders the recruits, once they have mounted their beds, to "pray," and, in unison, they offer up an ungodly doxology of praise for, and commitment to, their rifles. Camera and microphone travel from recruit to individual recruit, recording their faces, their shouts: Joker, Cowboy, Joker again, Pyle. Next day, on the parade deck, Hartman drills the platoon at the exacting manual of arms; his criticism of Pyle is relatively acerbic. That night, in the barracks, Hartman marches the men back and forth, all of them chanting: "This is my rifle; this is my gun. This is for fighting; this is for fun." With one hand, each grasps his rifle; with the other, each grasps, and rhythmically pulls, his genitals.

Disparities between these scenes and those in the novel are few. In either text, the recruits are made to name their rifles and to take them to bed (Hasford 13; 22). Hartman's speech, in fact, referencing the generic "Mary Jane Rottencrotch," is appropriated almost verbatim from the original (13). Like Hartman, Gerheim discriminates ritualistically between a rifle and a gun (12). The scene in which the men pray, however, has been somewhat altered. At an equivalent stage of the novel, they are required not to pray, but to sing "The Marines' Hymn" (10). The activity can very nearly be seen as wholesome, as something that Boy Scouts might do. But saying a prayer in which one promises bluntly to shoot one's enemy jostles the viewer into what a colonel will later tell Joker is a "hardball world." Actually, the fictional recruits do recite the so-called "Rifleman's Creed," but the recitation happens later in the narrative, and the words are significantly different from those in the adaptation. "My rifle is human, even as I," the creed goes, "because it is my life. Thus I will learn it as a brother" (23). In the film, the recruits' humanity is expressly denied—"You are not even human fucking beings," Hartman insists—and they are not to learn their rifles as a brother, but as a woman: a lover. It seems that as the film mitigates the novel's physical violence, it fortifies the violence of words and ideas; the skewed reality of the source, though reconfigured, is kept skewed.

Pyle as Albatross

In this phase of the narrative, the film centers on Pyle's ineptitude, and what it means to the rest of the platoon. The men are now driven through a series of field exercises intended both to test and to strengthen them. They march on the parade deck, then climb up and down knotted ropes. As Hartman rants at them, they swing through an "armstretcher" obstacle, negotiate a wooden tower, and drub each other with pugil sticks—Pyle gets beaten to the ground. At the next obstacle, a succession of suspended, horizontal logs, Joker swiftly bounds over; Pyle fails miserably. The chinning bar defeats him too: he is unable to execute even one pull-up. He makes it to the top of the next obstacle, a giant ladder, but, weakened with fear, cannot get over. Screaming, Hartman vows to emasculate him so he "cannot contaminate the rest of the world." During an accelerated forced march, Pyle appears on the brink of collapse and is helped along by Joker; again, Hartman badgers him. At last, Pyle falls in the midst of a mud obstacle, and must be assisted by Joker and Cowboy.

The germ of this sequence, and little more, may be found in the novel. We understand that the fictional recruits must master a "Confidence Course," fighting with pugil sticks, and bayonet training (Hasford 14). One aspect of the Confidence Course is the "slide-for-life": a rope strung at a 45-degree angle across a muddy pond. Pyle repeatedly slips from the rope and plummets into the water; once, he has to be rescued (14). Hasford's description is, to say the least, Spartan, and the reader has only a sketchy notion of what the men are suffering, of the sergeant's overbearing presence, and of any drama that may—or should—be building. But the film brings the novel's emaciated paragraphs to raucous life. The recruits yell and groan and perspire. Hartman continues to bellow his "Rabelaisian vituperations" (Kroll, "1968" 64). Most crucially, the film is setting up, more clearly and effectively than the book, the conflict between Pyle and his peers, and Pyle and his sergeant.

Before dawn on a Sunday, Hartman and two assistants stride into the squad bay to wake the recruits. Hartman orders Cowboy and Joker to clean the "head"; he wants it so sanitary that the Virgin Mary herself would be "proud to go in there and take a dump." When Hartman asks Joker if he believes in the Virgin Mary, Joker replies that he does not. Offended, Hartman calls Joker a "goddam communist heathen," backhands him crisply, and strongly suggests, on pain of further punishment, that Joker rethink his theology. Joker respectfully declines, and offers the opinion that the sergeant would beat him more severely if he were to reverse himself. On hearing this response, Hartman summarily relieves Snowball as squad leader and replaces him with Joker, whose intrepidness has impressed Hartman. Further, Pyle is to bunk with Joker, who will teach him how to become a Marine.

Though roughly similar, the fictional and adapted versions of this scene are distinguished by small but appreciable contrasts in rhetoric. In the novel, Joker is convinced that Gerheim's question has no correct answer, and that trying to locate one will result only in a more violent beating—but he does not articulate his belief (Hasford 8). Since we may read his thoughts, he is not obligated to. But

Recalling his adjustments to Quilty, Kubrick gives the adversarial sergeant an expanded presence in the film.

having the film Joker voice his belief not only satisfies the demands of the medium, it provides a demonstration of his grace under pressure, hence justifying Hartman's decision. (Gerheim's decision seems more beholden to intuition: "Have you seen the light?" he asks Joker mystically. "The white light? The great light? The guiding light—do you have the vision?" [9].) More of a renegade than his film counterpart, the original Joker resists the promotion, and also resists the prospect of bunking with Pyle (9–10); the film Joker, though impish, is more obedient, more conventional. By keeping silent, he confirms that he is a recognizable leader, however reluctant. The text confirms it as well, by sustaining his lofty status: in the novel, the whimsical Gerheim soon demotes Joker when the recruit falls out of a tree during war games, and replaces him with Cowboy (12). Though less bullying physically than Gerheim—the film sergeant does not take men into the shower stall and batter them—Hartman continues to be more outrageous (8). One notices a streak of blasphemy in his harangues. At reveille, he tells the recruits to "drop [their] cocks and grab [their] socks"; in his next breath he reminds them that today is Sunday and "divine worship is at zero eight hundred." The counterpoint is stunning, but no more so than his staunch defense of the Virgin Mary while imagining that she might proudly "take a dump" in a Parris Island latrine. Regardless of how one reads these messages—Denby finds Hartman "hideously funny" but "morally repugnant"—one must conclude that the sergeant's presence is more dynamic here than in the source (54).

Joker's gentle, patient tutoring of Pyle begins without delay. He shows Pyle how to assemble a rifle, and how to lace his boots. Perched atop the towering ladder-like obstacle that caused Pyle to freeze earlier, Joker talks his apprentice over, giving him step-by-step encouragement. He next shows Pyle how properly to make his bed, and how to execute specific movements in the manual of arms. We see that Joker's efforts are having a beneficial effect when Pyle is able, under Hartman's icy stare, to breeze through an obstacle and to march efficiently. The venue now moves to the rifle range, where Hartman lectures on the need for the recruits to cultivate their "killer instincts." If they do not, he warns, they may hesitate at the "moment of truth." Like his fellows, Pyle seems attentive and enthusiastic; his attitude does not waver as Hartman, chanting cadences, double-times the platoon through the streets.

The film's handling of these scenes differs from the novel's in both style and substance. Hasford continues to favor diegesis over mimesis—predominantly, we are *told* what happens, not shown. For example, Joker states: "I teach [Pyle] everything I know, from how to lace his black combat boots to the assembly and disassembly of the M-14 semi-automatic shoulder weapon" (Hasford 11). The events do not unfurl before our mind's eye as they could and perhaps should. Even the sergeant's "killer instinct" speech is conveyed indirectly: "Sergeant Gerheim explains that it is important for us to understand that it is our killer instinct which must be harnessed if we expect to survive in combat. Our rifle is only a tool ..." (13). The film's representation of these events in the moment stems largely from the nature of the medium, but there is also a creative rhetoric involved. Which if any words might be employed, the arrangement of the players, their expressions, the backdrops—all these issues are resolved through conscious decisions made chiefly by Kubrick. Again, a very lean piece of fiction is being filled out for the screen. Apart from style, the story itself is given a different slant by the film. In the novel, Joker's touching fraternalism is missing:

> [Pyle] looks at me. "I'm sure glad you're helping me, Joker. You're my friend. I know I'm slow. I've always been slow. Nobody ever helped me...."
> I turn away. "That sounds like a personal problem," I say. I keep my eyes on my weapon [11].

What is more, the original Pyle shows no tangible signs of improvement under Joker's tutelage (11–15). By having Joker offer a facsimile of friendship, and by having Pyle respond, the film prepares to raise a pair of artfully loaded questions: Would it not be especially galling to Joker and the others if, under these circumstances, Pyle were to betray them, not through native incompetence, but through deliberate selfishness? And would not such a betrayal rightly demand retribution?

In the barracks, Hartman inspects the hands and feet of the recruits, who, wearing just their white T-shirts and undershorts, stand at attention on their footlockers. He notices that Pyle's footlocker is unlocked—a violation of the rules, and valid cause for Hartman to fulminate. Ordering Pyle off the footlocker, Hartman tears it apart and discovers a jelly doughnut—two more violations, since food is not allowed in the barracks, and since Pyle, a "disgusting fatbody," is forbidden from eating doughnuts. Hartman now addresses the other recruits, advising them that, henceforth, when Pyle transgresses, they—and not Pyle—will be punished; it will be their responsibility to help Hartman motivate Pyle. To underscore his point, he orders all but Pyle to do pushups; Pyle must stand in their midst and consume his doughnut. Next morning, Pyle seems to have backslid further: Joker, tight-lipped and remote, must help him dress. An abrupt cut to the training field shows most of the men performing squat-thrusts, counting them off, evidently as punishment. Conspicuously, Pyle sits by himself along the periphery, his cap turned backwards, his thumb in his mouth.

Once more, Kubrick has reshaped the narrative in ways that deserve attention. Pyle's offense and the sergeant's reaction to it are decidedly different in the two texts. The original Pyle forgets to shave one morning; Joker, fatigued and mentally scattered, forgets to remind him. Gerheim spies the deficiency, and takes punitive action (Hasford 15–16). One registers that the fictional Pyle's offense is not willful; he does not consciously decide against shaving. Moreover, Joker, who is himself negligent, must share some of the blame. In the film, Pyle acts knowingly and surreptitiously—culpability therefore goes to him alone. Gerheim's response to Pyle's slovenliness is to force Pyle's head into a urine-filled toilet bowl and hold it there until he nearly drowns (15–16). Hartman's course—ordering Pyle to eat the doughnut, and the others to do pushups—is less crude, less violent, and yet it also does more to unite the resentful platoon against Pyle. In the film, right and wrong are more readily discerned; hence the story is simpler, its logic easier to follow. As before, one observes minor adjustments in how the sergeant and Joker have been constructed. Gerheim makes no hard-hitting speech about group punishment; his strategy merely asserts itself: "Now," Joker narrates, "whenever [Pyle] makes a mistake, Sergeant Gerheim does not punish [him]. He punishes the whole platoon. He excludes [Pyle] from the punishment" (16). But Hartman, not unlike Kubrick's Quilty, commands a bigger moiety of the narrative. Joker, too, continues along his own new path, his toward a more mainstream set of values. Even though annoyed, this latter Joker helps Pyle get dressed. The original refuses to speak to Pyle, and draws away from him (16); it is ignoble behavior, and tends to short-circuit our powers of identification.

Late at night, the darkened barracks stir quietly to life. Anonymous hands place a towel on a bed, and then a bar of soap on the towel. The hands now fold the towel over the soap, creating a weapon something like a blackjack. Joker slips from his bed, and, making certain Pyle is asleep, signals the other recruits, who also emerge from their beds. They creep toward the unsuspecting Pyle and surround him. Cowboy inserts a gag into the victim's mouth as his confederates stretch a blanket over Pyle's body, preventing his escape. The men not involved in pinioning Pyle sweep past him, striking him with their soap-weapons; his anguished screams are muffled by the gag. Joker, who has delayed his own assault, now thrashes Pyle six times, hard, on the chest and belly. Releasing the gag, Cowboy says: "Remember, it's just a bad dream, fat boy." He and the others return to their beds as Pyle sits up, sobbing in shock and pain. His face a mask, Joker covers his ears with his hands.

What happens in the film is not dissimilar from what happens in the novel. At midnight on the first night of the seventh week of training, the platoon gives Pyle a "blanket party" (Hasford 16). The attack, involving one hundred recruits, is implemented as in the film, although perhaps with a more dire effect on Pyle: by the time Joker takes his turn, Pyle has stopped screaming and stopped moving (16–17). Nevertheless, Joker beats him "harder and harder," and, when he feels a pang of remorse, beats him harder still (17). But if anything sets the film scene apart from the original, it is Kubrick's superbly haunting atmospheric touches. The lighting is gray on gray, yielding a nightmarish grisaille; the music, a slow cycle of two notes, seems to have been composed on another planet. In the calculated dimness, and against the dread music, the men in their skivvies move like maleficent ghosts. For once, we empathize with Pyle (as we do not in the book), even though it was his flouting of the rules that has led to the beating. Because Joker is generally more civilized in the film, his actions now are more unsettling to us. Even as the Vietnam War dredged up difficult moral questions, the film here prods us to ask a few about Joker. Is his participation in the attack morally defensible? If so, why does he cover his ears at the sound of Pyle's whimpering? If not, what further corrosions may come to his soul as the story progresses?

Pyle, Born Again

In this segment, Pyle, influenced by the blanket party, undergoes a dark metamorphosis that leads to his becoming a "defective instrument" (Hasford 31). After a significant blackout, the action resumes on the parade deck as Hartman drills the recruits. Pyle performs impeccably, though when Hartman asks rote questions of the group—Do we love our beloved Corps? What makes the grass grow? What do we do for a living?—Pyle does not lend his voice to the chorus of (also rote) answers. He just stares vaguely and silently ahead. We next see the recruits assembled in rows of bleachers, outdoors, beneath a threatening sky. Standing before them, the sergeant dilates on the sharpshooting achievements of mass murderer Charles Whitman and Kennedy assassin Lee Harvey Oswald, both of whom, he stresses with pride, obtained their skills in the Marines. Unnoticed, Pyle continues to stare ahead vacantly, wearing the facies of some deep distraction. Inside the barracks, Hartman leads the men in singing "Happy Birthday" to Jesus in commemoration of Christmas. The song finished, Hartman declares that "God has a hard-on for Marines, because [they] kill everything [they] see." In tribute to God, he adds, the Marines keep heaven packed with fresh souls.

Much of this sequence is taken faithfully from the source, and yet much has been invented or modified. The question-and-answer session on the parade deck, in which we first notice a change in Pyle's affect and behavior, comes straight from the novel, as does the sergeant's remark that a recruit may "give [his] heart to Jesus, but [his] ass belongs to the Corps." (Curiously, although Gerheim asserts that Marines existed before God [Hasford 19], Hartman supposes that God predates Marines—a bit of an inconsistency in a character who so cherishes blasphemy.) Hartman's paean to a pair of America's most infamous riflemen is rooted in the book, but, like many other aspects of the original, has been expanded and colorized. Hasford's coverage of the incident is so skimpy as to be hardly perceptible:

> On the third day of our seventh week we move to the rifle range and shoot holes in paper targets. Sergeant Gerheim brags about the marksmanship of ex–Marines Charles Whitman and Lee Harvey Oswald [17].

In his rendering of the scene, Kubrick has endowed it with foreboding (the storm cloud in the sky, and the one obscuring Pyle's face), humor (Snowball's "book suppository" malapropism), sound, movement, visuality, and the ongoing enlarged presence of the sergeant. The "Happy Birthday" song is new, and marvelously suited to Hartman's reverent-irreverent style: the song enhances his kooky, fist-swinging image, whereas something more sublunary and traditional—"Silent Night," let us say—would have chafed against it. The song also provides him with a springboard to his "God has a hard-on for Marines" discourse. Those bizarre observations actually belong, in the novel, to the battle-hardened Joker (150); obviously, his refurbished persona would not accommodate them. Too mind-fogging to be excluded from the film, Kubrick assigns them to Hartman, where they find the perfect match. One might also mention that Kubrick omits a suicide attempt by one Private Perkins (18–19). Potent enough to have been included, the attempt might have siphoned our attention away from Pyle. Absent Perkins and his slashed wrists, the film is able, cleanly and unequivocally, to present Pyle as the sole problem recruit.

In the barracks, seated on their footlockers, the recruits clean their rifles. Along with Joker, we pick up Pyle's whispering, lover's voice as he coos to his weapon: "It's been swabbed, and wiped. Everything is clean. Beautiful. So that it slides perfectly. Nice. Everything cleaned. Oiled. So that your action is beautiful. Smooth, Charlene." Joker looks at him with concern, but says nothing. Mopping the latrine, he does mention Pyle's eccentricity to Cowboy; both men suspect that Pyle is a "Section Eight." Joker now casually states that he wants to "slip [his] tube-steak into [Cowboy's] sister"; Cowboy's low-key reaction is equally casual. On the rifle range, Hartman hovers behind Pyle, who fires his weapon at a distant target; as Pyle reloads, Hartman sincerely compliments his prowess. Later, on the parade deck, Hartman inspects the recruits. Examining Joker's rifle, Hartman demands of him: "What's your sixth General Order?" Joker is unable to answer satisfactorily. Moving to Pyle, the sergeant pelts him with questions, all of which Pyle answers accurately and authoritatively. A pleased Hartman pays him a second compliment, telling Pyle that he has been "born again, hard."

The foregoing sequence is characterized primarily by omissions, though it also features one key expansion of the source material. In the world of the novel, Joker's off-color remark to Cowboy is just part of a longstanding routine in which these friends indulge; Joker's foray and Cowboy's reply—each given breath for the "hundredth time"—are always the same (Hasford 20). The film reduces their badinage to a single exchange. Coming as it does from nowhere, and in the wake of the latest development with Pyle, it drops on us as quite a non sequitur, oddly humorous and pleasantly dislocated, like many other aspects of the text. Other omissions involve the sergeant, who, in the novel, is aware that Pyle is at least mildly disturbed. When the recruit withdraws into a shell of silence, Gerheim counsels him, noting that the Marine Corps motto, *Semper Fidelis*, means "always faithful," and that "gung ho" is Chinese for "working together" (18). Indeed, Gerheim is made aware that Pyle talks to his rifle; he thereupon informs the others that Pyle is unquestionably a Section Eight, and, irritated, orders the gabbing men to belay any further scuttlebutt about the matter (21). Of course Hartman, who is structured more as a force than as a person, a thing to be feared, obeyed, and appeased, does not stoop to informal conversation with the recruits. To have had him mixing with the men, expressing a personal opinion about a recruit's mental state, would have lowered his station. More, it would have upset the narrative's balance, which depends on a group of ordinary men's coming to terms with the blunt, killer culture of the Marines, as embodied by Hartman. The expansion relates to Pyle, whose advancement Hasford conveys by flat asseverations channeled through Joker: Pyle "has become a model recruit.... His manual of arms is flawless now.... [He] cleans his weapon more than any recruit in the platoon" (18). But Kubrick allows us see this advancement for ourselves, and in catchy detail; the director's technique, more cinematic, is also more convincing.

As he has before, Hartman double-times the recruits through the streets of Parris Island. On this occasion, he calls the following cadence:

> I don't want no teenage queen;
> I just want my M-14.
> If I die in the combat zone,
> Box me up and ship me home.
> Pin my medals upon my chest;
> Tell my mom I've done my best.

In full combat gear, the recruits emerge from a clearing in the forest, then charge aggressively across an open field. Joker's voice-over observes that graduation is only a few days away—the men are "salty"—and allows that the Marine Corps does not want robots, but killers. We cut to graduation day, and, in the barracks, Hartman welcomes the men to the brotherhood of Marines. Over shots of the graduation ceremony, he notes that most of the recruits will go to Vietnam, and that some will not return. Later, he announces their new assignments. Cowboy will join the infantry, as will Pyle, who by now seems barely functional. Joker will pursue "basic military journalism," a peculiarity that elicits something like bluff humor from Hartman: "You think you're Mickey Spillane? ... You're not a writer; you're a killer."

On the whole, the film and the novel are, at this juncture, well-synchronized. Kubrick does shave away certain details of the fictional graduation: Pyle is selected as "outstanding recruit," congratulated by the Commanding General, and awarded a citation (Hasford 24). Joker is promoted to Private First Class, and Cowboy is chosen to carry the platoon guidon (24). In eliminating these items, Kubrick keeps the novel's spirit and the film's celerity, and avoids the potential awkwardness of dwelling too much on Pyle, who has crossed over into psychosis. The fictional recruits chant no cadences, but they do sing a song whose macabre lyrics are echoed by Hartman: "Say good-bye to Dad and Mom. / Hey, Marine.... / You're gonna die in Vietnam. / Hey, Marine, yeah!" (25). Joker's comment concerning the Corps' desire for killers is excerpted directly from the book (19), and, like the cadence (or the song), is critical to the theme. The text has repeatedly, if prematurely, identified the recruits as killers; in effect, it is asking us to consider the possibility. Might they kill in Vietnam, and, if so, with what consequences? Might one of the men elect to kill before going to Vietnam—before he has received official sanction? The sergeant's gibe at Joker is hinted at in the novel: "Sergeant Gerheim is disgusted by the fact that I am to be a combat correspondent and not a grunt" (25). By expanding and animating this disgust, the film accomplishes two ends. First, it continues to pound on the "killer" theme: "You're not a writer; you're a killer." Second, the manner of Hartman's criticism—lightly bantering—makes him seem, for once, almost human. Perhaps what we have seen of his personality has been largely an act; perhaps he is more, or less, than he seems. Perhaps, we may think, he is just a mortal after all, in which case his earlier statement, "Marines die; that's what we're here for," will soon be revealed as devastating Kubrickian irony.

It is, Joker tells us, the recruits' last night on the island; he has drawn fire watch. Patrolling the squad bay with a flashlight, he hears a dull thud that brings him cautiously to the latrine. He pushes open the door, and, inside, finds Pyle seated on a toilet, amid the shadows, loading a magazine for his M-14 rifle. Pyle bids Joker hello, but his voice is distorted, his expression subhuman. Joker gently warns him that if Hartman catches them in the latrine, they will both be in a "world of shit." Pyle replies vehemently that he already is, then stands and begins executing the manual of arms, punctuating his movements with shouts. He now inserts the magazine into his weapon, and commences screaming the rifle prayer. The commotion rouses the others, including Hartman, who enters the latrine in a rage. He flings one heated question after another at Joker before Joker advises him that Pyle has "locked and loaded" a full magazine. Lowering his voice, Hartman orders Pyle to place the rifle on the deck; instead, Pyle aims it at Hartman. The sergeant abruptly reverts to form, bellowing insults at Pyle. Without a word, Pyle shoots Hartman through the chest, toppling him backwards. For a moment, Pyle trains the rifle on Joker, who is fearfully but resolutely standing still. At last Pyle reseats himself, puts the rifle's muzzle in his own mouth, and fires. Gouts of blood spray the wall behind him.

The climax of the narrative's first phase, this sequence has been reformulated and reduced from the original. Perhaps the most obvious deviation lies with the setting: in the novel, the disturbance occurs not in the latrine, but in the squad bay, near Pyle's bed (Hasford 26–27). The supernumerary Marines all watch what happens, and, after Hartman is dead, some of them try to calm Pyle: "Go easy, Leonard," says Cowboy (30), using a line that gets displaced to the film Joker. But, as he does in *The Shining* with Jack and Grady, Kubrick transfers a singeing encounter from an open area to a lavatory. Though, in *Full Metal Jacket,* there may be some resonance between the new site and the catch phrase "a world of shit," the greater effect is, as before, to isolate the principals. Actors Vincent D'Onofrio (Pyle) and Lee Ermey (Hartman) are accorded a final turn in the light, and the pitch of the narrative is raised an extra notch. One also notices that the fictional Pyle is, by his words and actions, more manifestly deranged than the film version: he not only speaks to his rifle, he supplies a (woman's) voice—à la Norman, in Hitchcock's *Psycho*—whereby his rifle seems to speak to him (26). Field-stripping the weapon, he says: "This is the first time I've ever seen her naked," and prattles about her "pretty" trigger guard and her "beautiful" connector assembly (27). Yet the film Pyle is no less impressive in his lunacy, and the effect is achieved largely by the quality of his voice—almost narcotized to begin, then wild and booming—and by the monstrous look on his face. Kubrick has subordinated words to sounds and images. He has also shortened the length of the scene, erasing, in particular, the original's strange coda. In the novel, after Pyle has killed himself, Joker extinguishes the overhead lights and orders the others to get back into their beds (31–32). Caressing his own rifle, "Vanessa," he fantasizes that blood is pouring from its barrel, that the blood now coalesces into tiny red spiders, that the sleeping Marines are werewolves (32–33). Rich in symbolism, this envoy simply makes no sense on a literal level. In excising it, Kubrick maintains the film's coherence, and also upholds our impression of Joker as a relatively normal person: an initiate who is rapidly losing his innocence, but not a callous blood-lover who is only slightly more sane than Pyle.

Vietnam

Exposition

The numbing catastrophe in the latrine gives way to a blackout that presently dissolves to a daytime street scene in urban South Vietnam. Non-diegetic music obtrudes in the form of Nancy Sinatra's "These Boots Are Made for Walking." We follow the undulating prance of a Vietnamese prostitute as she crosses the busy street to a sidewalk table where a more hirsute Joker sits with another Marine, Rafterman. When the girl offers them her services, Joker, interested, negotiates the price downward; Rafterman snaps pictures of the two standing together. Suddenly a young Vietnamese man accosts Rafterman from behind, snatches his camera, and tosses it to an accomplice on a motorbike. Derisively, the thief exhibits a flurry of martial arts moves before climbing behind his colleague to drive away. As the two Marines stroll across the grounds of their military base, Rafterman complains about the ingratitude of the Vietnamese people and expresses his hunger to see combat. Joker, who evidently has some leverage in determining his friend's orders, tells him that, for Rafterman's own well-being, he will be given no "trigger time."

Kubrick has made no secret of his hope to transcend the timetempered conventions of mainstream cinematic storytelling. "The thing I'd really like to do," he has stated, "is explode the narrative structure of movies. I want to do something earthshaking" (Kroll, "1968" 65). One might guess, having absorbed *Full Metal Jacket*'s extraordinary flash-forward to the tumult of Vietnam, that Kubrick has, to a degree, realized his ambition. In reality, he has simply matched the gross structure of his film to that of the novel, which also leaps to a months-ahead, continents-away future. In less radical ways, however, he does, starting with the watershed blackout, depart from his source on a regular and freewheeling basis. Though one would probably not call his latter approach "earthshaking," it is rather liberal, and recalls his efforts in *The Shining*.

To begin the film's second movement, Kubrick omits material found in the novel and inserts new material. He also preserves one notable strand of the original—Rafterman's desire to "go out into the field" (Hasford 42–43). This retention is significant since Rafterman's eventual journey into the abominations of war will in some ways parallel Joker's, their similar experiences reinforcing each other thematically. Omitted from the film are Joker and Rafterman's visit to a theater to laugh at John Wayne in *The Green Berets,* and their subsequent visit to the USO, where they read letters written by children from back "in the World" (37–44). At their first stop, Joker is briefly reunited with Cowboy, and meets other members of the Lusthog Squad: Animal Mother, Alice, Donlon, Stutten, Doc Jay, T.H.E. Rock, and Crazy Earl. By withholding the encounter until later, Kubrick simplifies his project, limiting the amount of information dispensed at one time. The Marines' second stop, to read the warm and innocent letters, shows that Rafterman still has feelings that may be touched; Joker spurns the letters as "shoes for the dead, who do not walk" (44). The omission saves time, and saves the film Joker's image; we know him as flippant and cynical, but not as wholly unregenerate. What actually does serve to open the Vietnam segment—the prostitute, the stolen camera—is not part of the novel. But it tallies with the book's tone, and quickly evokes the paradox of fighting for a nation whose need to be saved is debatable.

Joker and Rafterman take their places at a round-table editorial meeting of the Marine newspaper; the meeting is conducted by the disingenuous and arrogant Lieutenant Lockhart. When Joker asks about a rumor that the Tet cease-fire may be canceled, Lockhart dismisses the possibility as "rear-echelon paranoia," and ridicules the Vietnamese culture. Lockhart assigns Rafterman to cover a visit from Ann-Margret, specifying that he wants the photographs as prurient as possible. He next makes a series of niggling suggestions regarding some of the correspondents' copy. Reading a story written by Joker, he asks pointedly: "Where's the weenie?"— meaning the report of the enemy dead. He reminds Joker that the paper runs only two types of story: "winning of hearts and minds" and "winning the war," the second of which is always tied to enemy casualties. Joker replies that, in this instance, he witnessed none, whereupon Lockhart orders him to rewrite the story using some imagination. Joker carefully mocks the lieutenant, and a tension between the two men asserts itself.

No such meeting occurs in the novel. While the original Joker is indeed a correspondent—he tells us he is (Hasford 37), and refers to his assignments—he never actually plies his trade in front of the reader(37; 45; 58). By affording us a glimpse of Joker's performing in the role of reporter, the film again affirms its bias toward visual concreteness. In the source, as in the film, Joker's relation to his work is irreverent and ironic. He seems amused that his commanding officer, Major Lynch, has decided that a "really inspiring piece" could be written about Hill 327, the first position permanently occupied by American forces (37). Finished with the story, Joker wryly proclaims it a triumph: "It takes talent to convince people that war is a beautiful experience" (45). He soon confronts another superior, Captain January, about the mysterious suppression of an earlier story Joker submitted concerning an American howitzer crew that annihilated a squad of NVA with a "beehive round," a device judged inhumane by the Geneva Convention (58). Discarding these incidents, the film still conveys Joker's rebellious and provocative stance—and it does so in one quick, concentrated exchange; Kubrick has successfully economized the narrative. Lockhart, incidentally, does not appear in the novel, just as Lynch and January do not appear in the film. The effete film lieutenant is essentially an amalgam of the two fictional officers.

As dusk settles, and fireworks light the sky, Joker's voice-over tells us that Tet, the Vietnamese lunar New Year celebration, is upon us. Inside a hootch, Joker, Rafterman, and other Marines are lolling about in their bunks. When Joker, stretching, says he needs to get back "into the shit" to alleviate his boredom, Payback pokes sophomoric fun at him. Joker has never been in action, Payback claims; he lacks the "thousand-yard stare" that all field Marines reputedly acquire. Payback mentions his own trying experience in Operation Hastings, only to have Chili dispute that Payback was even in the country during Hastings. Now mortar shells burst nearby and the lights flicker; the Marines grab their weapons and scramble out into the night. A siren blares and flames erupt as we follow Joker into a bunker, where he mans an M-60 machine gun. An enemy truck breaks through the perimeter gate, and the Marines open fire on the vehicle, causing it to explode. NVA troops rush in behind its burning carcass, to be cut down by more automatic fire from the Marines. Gradually the fighting dwindles.

This *Iliad*-like sequence, in which the Marines alternate talking and warring, represents a melding together of two separate episodes from the novel. The first, originally positioned just after Joker's writing of the Hill 327 story, finds him and Rafterman perched on the roof of the ISO hootch in the First Marine Division Headquarters area near Da Nang (Hasford 44–46). Enjoying the fireworks, they are startled when a rocket "hits the deck fifty yards away" (46). They fall into a sandbagged bunker, arm themselves, and watch as a battle unfolds around them. Neither man takes any stalwart action; no truck crashes through a gate; and no enemy soldiers are seen (46–47). By contrast, the film particularizes the skirmish—it takes on a distinctive, captivating shape—and gives Joker a noticeably active participation in its management and outcome: as the text's central figure, he does not merely watch and wait. The second fictional episode is situated later in the narrative, by which time Joker and Rafterman are in Phu Bai, trading gossip in the ISO enlisted men's hootch. The barbs that fly back and forth among the men, and especially between Joker and Payback, are much the same as in the film (63–66). For the purposes of adaptation, the scene has, however, been cut and rearranged. Dropped are Payback's time-consuming philosophisms on retribution and atheism (64–65), and Chili's morose prediction that Joker will be killed in action (66). Joker's comments about being bored come near the end of the colloquy, not at the start, as in the film (66). But in either case, they provide a rhetorical bridge to combat, and offer the sly lesson that boredom is not always a condition to be scorned. Macroscopically, the film's blending of the two episodes contracts the narrative; worthy material is kept, but compressed into a denser package.

In the morning, Lockhart paces around the meeting table summarizing for his weary correspondents just what has happened. The enemy has violated the cease-fire and launched an offensive all over the country. In Saigon, the United States Embassy has been overrun, while Khe Sanh is preparing to be overrun. The strategic situation is grim, and the public relations dynamic is even worse: Walter Cronkite is about to suggest that the "war is now unwinnable." Following a pregnant pause, Joker asks if this fiasco means that Ann-Margret is no longer coming. Exasperated, Lockhart orders Joker to leave for Phu Bai posthaste, and, as an afterthought, to remove his peace symbol. Rafterman requests permission to accompany Joker; ignoring Joker's objection, Lockhart grants the request.

The aftermath of the Tet surprise is substantially the same from text to text. In the novel, Major Lynch updates the correspondents, orders Joker to Phu Bai, and permits Rafterman to go with him (Hasford 47–48). But, on a more micro level, two differences stand out in how the narratives are shaded. During combat, the film Joker appears tense; during the postmortem meeting, he seems disaffected. A much tougher and more perverse breed, the fictional Joker reacts sneeringly to the confusion in the "carnival" of the ISO:

> The New Guys are about to wet their pants. Everyone is talking.... Most of these guys have never been in the shit. Violence doesn't excite them the way it excites me because they don't understand it the way I do. They're afraid. Death is not yet their friend [47].

Death, one observes, is not yet the film Joker's friend, either. He is still adjusting to the war; he feels a discomfort, which we are asked to share. Though he is no doubt cheekier than the typical viewer, he is not yet much harder, and our identification with him is certainly possible. The second difference between the texts involves a demonstration of the film Joker's cheek, and how the moment fits into the narrative's proairetic line, its chain of causality (Thompson 39). In the novel, Lynch sends Joker to Phu Bai because the move would seem logical—not to punish him or to be rid of him (Hasford 48). But the film Joker is curtly excused because of his insubordination: his inappropriate (and newly written) riposte about Ann-Margret. The film's tactic is therefore more dramatic, and more instructive. Command decisions in Vietnam are not necessarily indebted to logic, and Joker, by opposing the corrupt official mentality, is exceptional, independent, perhaps even admirable.

Hue, Cowboy, and the Lusthog Squad

Borne by helicopter, Joker and Rafterman travel toward a landing zone near Hue. En route, a maniacal doorgunner, bawling "Get some! Get some!" fires an M-60 at terror-stricken Vietnamese peasants who scurry through a field. When Joker, disapproving, asks him how he can shoot women and children, he replies: "Easy. You just don't lead them so much." Rafterman is ill—from the flight, the activity of the doorgunner, or both. The two correspondents land safely, secure directions, and begin walking briskly down a dusty road clogged with tanks, trucks, and soldiers, all on the move. Joker and Rafterman catch up with a Marine known as Touchdown, who happens to be Cowboy's platoon commander. Tagging along with him, they learn that the NVA are "dug in deep," and have been executing civilians. Touchdown, using a map, shows Joker where bodies might be found.

As much as any tract of the film, including its ending, this one is characterized by the enormity of its omissions; some 35 pages of the novel have been excluded or transposed (Hasford 49–83). At bottom, we simply do not see Joker and Rafterman in Phu Bai (though the film's seamless construction makes the elision virtually unnoticeable). Some of the items in the source that do not survive adaptation are gaudy. Leaving in a C-130 cargo plane with Rafterman, Joker recalls how his friend earned his sobriquet: drunk one night at the Thunderbird Club, he fell from the rafters and crashed through a general's table (49–50). Upon arrival in Phu Bai, Joker overcomes an imperious MP by brandishing an M-16 at him (53–54). Joker then encounters the Monopoly-obsessed Captain January—who promotes him against his will to sergeant—and wages his war of wits with Payback in the ISO hootch (57–60; 63–67). Desperate with ennui, Joker and his comrades trap some rats and set them afire; Joker kisses a dead rat, and Payback eats a crispy tail (67–70). Following an enemy mortar attack that leaves one Marine, Winslow, dead, Rafterman ceremoniously eats a piece of his flesh (71–74). Ultimately, Joker and Rafterman hitch a ride to Hue in a tank; the tank rolls over a young girl and a water buffalo—the girl's grandfather demands compensation for the loss of the water buffalo (77–79). While all these omissions promote narrational speed, some do more. The quantity of violence is reduced, and its sometimes weird nature curbed. Joker and Rafterman are presented as normal young men in a hostile environment, not as psychopaths in their own fiefdom Hastened, the story is also softened.

What we do see on-screen has been changed from the original in a number of ways. In the novel, the depraved doorgunner is "naked except for an unbuttoned Hawaiian sport shirt. On the Hawaiian sport shirt are a hundred yellow hula dancers" (Hasford 75). One conjectures that the man's inexplicable appearance, carried over to the film, would have diverted our attention away from his actions, and would have seemed less surrealistic than silly. The fictional doorgunner does not speak—though he does giggle (75)—and the film's chant of "Get some! Get some!" is originally uttered by Payback, who is gleefully celebrating the panic of the burning, dying rats (69). It is a queer and hypnotic phrase, invested perhaps with sexual overtones (Reaves 229), and one is pleased at its preservation. The remainder of the film doorgunner's ravings reminds us of war's senseless horrors; as the character himself puts it: "Ain't war hell?" Rafterman's queasiness, nonexistent in the book, sets up a visual continuum of hardihood, ranging from him to Joker in the middle to the doorgunner at the opposite extreme: we are invited to see each man's evolution (or devolution) under the influence of war. Finally, Cowboy's platoon commander, "Shortround" in the novel (Hasford 85), becomes "Touchdown" in the film; the latter name, with its intimations of heroism, is more ironic, since he is destined soon to die.

His expression pained and sorrowful, Joker peers down into an open grave at a neat row of lime-covered corpses. In voice-over, he observes that the dead know only one thing: "It is better to be alive." He turns now to a Lieutenant Cleves and asks how the massacre came about. Smiling for Rafterman's camera, Cleves answers that the NVA requested citizens to report for "political re-education"; those who complied were shot. The interview is cut short when a belligerent colonel strides over to Joker and upbraids him for wearing a peace symbol. Noting that Joker is also wearing the inscription "BORN TO KILL" on his helmet, the colonel demands to know if Joker is perpetrating a "sick joke." Joker's response touches on Carl Jung and the duality of man, prompting the mystified colonel to deliver a blustery, and hilarious, speech. "Inside every gook," he rumbles, "there is an American trying to get out. It's a hardball world, son. We've got to keep our heads until this peace craze blows over."

This scene conflates a pair of episodes from the novel—Joker's visit to a mass grave, and his separate brush with a colonel. Before merging them, the film trims, alters, and shuttles them about. Unlike the adaptation, the source contains two encounters with snipers: one in Hue, and one in the jungle near Khe Sanh. Originally, the incidents noted transpire between these encounters (Hasford 126–27; 134–39). Since the film involves just one sniper attack, and since that adventure is climactic, the subject scene—if it is to occur at all—must occur beforehand: any subsequent actions would smack of bathos. Positioned in the narrative as it is, the grave-and-colonel scene properly intensifies our impression of disorder and inversion. The film's moments at the graveside suggest that Joker is superior morally to most of those around him. We read the grief written on his face, and unavoidably notice the gulf between his manner and that of the publicity-minded Cleves and the picayune colonel—neither of whom is present in the novel's sister scene (126–27). As elsewhere, the film humanizes and valorizes Joker. Indeed, the fictional Joker clambers down into the grave and, "crushing the stiff bodies with [his] knee until dry bones crack," binds some corpses with demolition wire to contrive an atrocity photograph (127). Later, with Rafterman recently killed, Joker gets waylaid by a "poge" colonel while hitchhiking south on Route One toward Phu Bai (135). Their exchange is longer in the book than in the film, covering five and a fraction pages (134–39), and even more bizarre. Joker conceives the notion that the colonel is "going to bite [him] in the neck.... [The officer's] smile is cold. His skin is too white" (136). Concluding his tirade, he brings Joker to his jeep and shows him, dumped into the back seat, a lance corporal with puncture marks on his neck. Now the colonel grins, baring his "vampire fangs," and steps toward Joker, who intimidates him with a wooden bayonet (139). In recasting this sequence, Kubrick has kept its vital core, while shunning its hallucinogenic edges—evidently even absurdity has its practical limits.

In the courtyard of a ruined pagoda, Joker and Rafterman come upon Cowboy, who is shaving. The reunion is a cheery one, with the expected bawdy reference to Cowboy's sister. Indicating the unsightly gaggle of Marines lurking along the courtyard wall, Cowboy proudly introduces the "Lusthog Squad," one of whom is Animal Mother. Animal sports a machine gun, a double bandoleer, and a helmet that proclaims "I AM BECOME DEATH"; he immediately attempts to pick a fight with Joker, who, spouting juvenile humor, holds his ground. Cowboy and a black Marine named Eightball separate the two before anything but words can be thrown. Our attention is directed now to Crazy Earl, who, gesturing at a pallid figure sprawled in a chair, invites Rafterman to take a picture of his "bro'."

Dramatically, Crazy Earl snatches away the man's hat, revealing him to be a dead NVA soldier. He explains that today is the dead man's birthday—he is the "guest of honor" at the squad's "party"—and regrets that when the Marines return home, there will be no one around "worth shooting."

Outwardly a straight, simple scene, this one has undergone a galaxy of changes in advancing from novel to film. Its length and fullness have been cut drastically. Originally, the Lusthog Marines are tossing around stacks of piasters obtained when they blew up a safe at a railroad terminal (Hasford 87). They wax nostalgic about their fallen, one-time "honcho" Stumbling Stewey, and discuss the Montagnard tribesmen (88–89). Animal Mother appears bearing food; he receives a commendation for having stolen it from the Army, and a reprimand for his repeated sexual attacks on pubescent Vietnamese girls (89–91). Joker does an impression of Bob Hope and spins a garbled tale about a Marine who was half robot (94). In concert with these omissions, the film generally curtails any prolixity in the characters' comments, and shunts aside altogether Shortround/Touchdown, whose presence in the book is marked. Yet even as the scene is reduced, it is enhanced by material garnered from other sections of the novel. At one point in the source, for example, we read:

> Cowboy and I grab each other and wrestle and punch and pound each other on the back. We say, "Hey, you old motherfucker. How you been? What's happening? Been getting any? Only your sister. Well, better my sister than my mom, although mom's not bad" [39–40].

But the moment depicted takes place in a Da Nang theater, not on the outskirts of Hue. Similarly, other patches of dialog are taken from an interlude in the jungle, near the end of the story. Among the lines salvaged are: "Thank God for sickle cell" (158), "Here or there, samey-same [*sic*]" (159), and "We talk the talk, but we don't walk the walk" (160). By retaining much of the novel's language, the film also retains much of its flavor, and insinuates a uniformity even among the many changes. As before, one spies the adapted narrative's consciousness of the visual: in the novel, Cowboy is not shaving, since there is no need to isolate him; Crazy Earl's removal of the dead man's hat (actually, a "bush cover") is comparatively low-key (86; 89). Another visual addition is the slogan on Animal's helmet; a line from the *Bhagavad Gita* by way of J. Robert Oppenheimer, it owes more to Kubrick's cleverness than to Animal's, but is a sumptuous touch nonetheless.

Behind tanks, the Marines cautiously move across a field and toward the smoldering city of Hue. Several enemy mortar rounds explode, and Touchdown falls, fatally wounded. Regrouping behind Crazy Earl, the men swarm at the shattered buildings in the distance. As they draw near, Hand Job peeks from behind a wall, and is killed by a burst of automatic fire. The Marines instantly and massively return fire, blasting chunks from the building in front of them. Rafterman's hands quake as he tries to snap photographs. Gradually the assault slackens, then ceases, and the men reload. A line of enemy soldiers suddenly scuttles from the building to safety. When two stragglers attempt to follow, Crazy Earl guns them down, and permits himself to glow with satisfaction.

Again, the sequence in the film bears only a dim resemblance to its model in the source. A prime factor here is a radical split between the texts in the means of narration, even beyond what we would normally expect from the two media. In the novel, soon after the battle begins, Joker is knocked unconscious by the concussion from a rocket-propelled grenade (Hasford 101–5). As a result, he is oblivious to the bulk of what happens—not a propitious circumstance for a narrator. Hours later, he is briefed, as are we, by Cowboy and Rafterman (105–6). In avoiding this detour, Kubrick keeps the film's narration clean, direct, and exciting. Other differences betide as well. Because the film Joker stays conscious, we are not sidetracked into his frivolous dream in which the three components of his being—mind, body, and spirit—yammer at each other (103–4). The list of casualties is different: in the novel, Shortround is dead, and so are Crazy Earl, T.H.E. Rock, and an unnamed radioman—it is a higher rate of loss (106–7). Hand Job does not exist fictionally; that he is created for the film only to be killed ensures that eulogistic comments will be, in light of his name, peculiar. Perhaps the most startling detail excluded from the film is the glaring suggestion that Shortround has been killed by the treacherous Animal

Mother (108; 121). The absence of any such suggestion in the film has little effect on our assessment of Animal, but it does simplify the story.

As Hue burns in the distance and the Marines sit resting in the foreground, a three-man camera crew creeps crab-like through the shot, filming. Stationary tanks fire at remote targets, and medical personnel go hurrying by. Some of the Marines familiar to us shout drivel at the passing microphone. Joker reprises his schizophrenic John Wayne line, and the others adopt the conceit that they are organizing a Hollywood spectacular. The scene shifts slightly, and now the members of the Lusthog Squad have formed a ring around their dead comrades, who lie side by side on the ground. Much as before, each survivor waits for the camera, then offers a succinct farewell. This pattern disintegrates as Animal Mother maintains he is fighting not for freedom but for "poontang," and Cowboy and Eightball reminisce over Hand Job's legendary habits of masturbation. Presently the diligent camera crew turns to an interview format to elicit the Marines' observations of the war. Each man uncovers a facet of his personality: Animal Mother, a modern Visigoth, suspects that Americans are "shooting the wrong gooks"; Cowboy condemns the lack of horses in Vietnam; and Joker claims he "wanted to meet interesting and stimulating people of an ancient culture and kill them. [He] wanted to be the first kid on [his] block to get a confirmed kill."

Although sensitive to the novel's content, Kubrick continues to redeploy it according to his own artistic purposes. The fictional Marines pretend they are engaged in "just a John Wayne movie" *before* the battle, not after (Hasford 98–99); it is a way of calming their nerves. By having the film Marines fantasize afterwards, Kubrick is able to infuse the prelude to the battle, and the battle itself, with a high and unbroken seriousness that enthralls us. The lightness that follows, complemented by the thumping garage-rock of the Trashmen, allows us to exhale; one is reminded of the porter scene in *Macbeth*. Adjustments equally deft may be seen in the men's adieu to those who have died. Donlon's and Eightball's comments are true to the source, but Joker's and Animal Mother's depart sharply. In the novel, Joker looks at Shortround and declares: "Well, you're short, sir," referring both to his time left and his height. He then acknowledges to the reader that "making a bad pun was a stupid thing to do" (108). A wiser and more amiable character, the film Joker stays silent. Contrarily, Animal says nothing in the book, but in the film snarls: "Better you than me." Joker, the hero, is made a jot nobler, while Animal, the antihero, is made a jot more bestial. In this vein, some of the remarks spoken over Touchdown or for the interviewer originate in the novel, but in other contexts. At the Da Nang theater, for instance, Cowboy complains that "there's not one horse in all of Vietnam" (41). Savoring his story on Hill 327, Joker addresses the reader: "[M]eet interesting, stimulating people of an ancient culture ... and kill them. Be the first kid on your block to get a confirmed kill" (45). Much later, in the jungle, Animal unburdens himself of the "poontang" speech almost exactly as in the film (159). Shying away from the letter of the original, Kubrick befriends its spirit and its language.

Clustered outside a wrecked theater, the Marines are pleased at the arrival, by motor scooter, of an ARVN soldier and his companion, a baby-faced prostitute. The soldier-pimp advises the men that she is available for any kind of sexual diversion they might fancy. He and Cowboy quickly settle the price: five dollars a man, with some ARVN rifles thrown in as sweetener. The girl has reservations about coupling with Eightball, expressing fears that he may be physically "too beaucoup." Miffed, then amused, Eightball persuades her to reconsider by exposing himself for her evaluation and reassurance. He moves to take her first, but Animal Mother asserts his primacy; he slaps Eightball's hand, pushes the girl toward the theater, and decrees, with as much geniality as the words will suffer: "All fucking niggers must fucking hang."

A continuation of the idle time between the exertions of war, this scene has no definite analog in the novel. Rather, it pulls together some of the themes and intimations that percolate through the source. We have seen that the fictional Lusthog Squad has no aversion to theaters (Hasford 38–43), and certainly one might presume the same to be true of Stanley Kubrick. Here, then, as in the book, are the Marines lounging at a theater—though this one has ceased to do any legal business. The original Joker instructs Rafterman, and us, that the ARVN are corrupt:

[A]ny time you can see [one] you are safe from Victor Charlie. The [ARVN] run like rabbits at the first sign of violence.... [They] are not stupid when they are doing something they enjoy, like stealing. [They] sincerely believe that jewels and money are essential military supplies.
....
Money *is* their government [82–83].

Finding his objective correlative, Kubrick in this case illustrates the point that the novel merely states. The scene also hints at Animal Mother's primitive sexual style, indicated fictionally by his assaults on underage girls (90–91), and by his deck of playing cards, which feature "Tijuana whores ... establishing meaningful relationships with donkeys and big dogs" (156). Like so many other lines, Joker's quip about not being able to "get a piece of hand" first appears in the novel's closing jungle scene (159).

The Sniper

In voice-over, Joker apprises us that the squad has been ordered to patrol through Hue; intelligence believes that the enemy has lately withdrawn to positions across the Perfume River, but this belief must now be confirmed. A welter of smoke, flames, and charred debris, the city looks like an outpost in hell, and the Marines, spread apart, step gingerly through the rubble. Explosions echo in the distance. Emerging from the gutted shell of a building, Crazy Earl picks up a stuffed toy, detonating a booby trap. Despite the ministrations of Doc Jay, Earl dies, and Cowboy is authorized by radio to take over as squad leader. He seems unsure of himself. Grinning, Joker offers his friend a word of encouragement.

This short sequence is dominated by two interworked tendencies common to adaptation: a bias toward visual display and a reduction in the original's verbosity. Hasford's description is minimalist, not to say anemic, throughout the novel, and he never does attempt anything like a full-scale delineation of Hue in its destruction. His narrator, Joker, mentions that

> F-4 Phantom jet fighters are dropping napalm, high explosives, and Willy Peter—white phosphorous. With bombs [the Americans] are expressing [themselves]; [they] are writing ... history in shattered blocks of stone.
> Black roses of smoke bloom in the Citadel [Hasford 97].

But Kubrick's own description—he resourcefully used an abandoned gasworks to represent Hue—is powerful and unremitting(Lacayo 14). Terrence Rafferty, who found the cinematography overly controlled, noted the "small, evenly burning orange fires, impeccably placed among the ruins in every composition" (98), and David Denby commented on the "artfully disarranged" piles of detritus (55). The baneful effects of war, however carefully orchestrated, permeate every shot, and tell a daunting story of their own. Likewise, we now understand why the film Crazy Earl is granted a minutely longer life than his fictional shadow: it is so he can be killed off more garishly, and more ironically—by a child's toy. On the other hand, a two-page conversation in which Cowboy confides his uncertainty to Joker, and Joker bucks him up, is slashed to just two lines of dialog: "I'm the new squad leader" and "I'll follow you anywhere, scumbag." Of course, the characters' facial expressions and the timbre of their voices counterbalance what is omitted.

Checking his map, Eightball, the point man, calls Cowboy aside to tell him that the squad is out of position: they must change directions. Cowboy advises the men of this necessity, and sends Eightball to scout ahead. From an open area amid an agglomeration of wasted buildings, Eightball signals the men that they may approach, just as a sniper fires from a window, wounding his thigh. Blood spurting, he screams, spins, and falls—all in slow motion. The Marines unleash a fusillade at the various buildings, and then watch in dismay as the unseen sniper hits Eightball a second time, in the arm. By radio, Cowboy requests tank support, but now the sniper hits Eightball a third time, in the foot. Returning fire against orders and bickering defiantly, the men are slipping from Cowboy's control. When the sniper wings Eightball a fourth time, the restive Doc Jay goes on an unsanctioned rescue attempt; he too is felled. Cowboy learns that any tank support will be delayed and orders the squad to prepare to pull back. Animal Mother objects stridently to this plan and, as Doc Jay is wounded a second time, stages his own maverick rescue mission, charging at the gray buildings with his M-60 blazing. Doc bravely tries to pinpoint the sniper's location, and is instantly killed, along with Eightball, for his effort. Shouting, Animal indicates that the squad may advance; Cowboy hesitates, but then takes some men, including Joker and Rafterman, with him to join Animal. Still uncertain of what to do, Cowboy asks again for the radio, and accepts it while standing before a yawning hole in a wall. The sniper shoots him through the hole—like the others, Cowboy falls in slow motion—and he dies a moment later in Joker's arms.

As mentioned, the novel contains two distinct sniper episodes, whereas the film has only one. But it would be less accurate to deduce that Kubrick has discarded an episode than to appreciate that he has combined the original couple into a film hybrid. The first fictional sniper strikes in Hue while Joker is unconscious; Cowboy later recounts what happened. Walking point, T.H.E. Rock had his foot shot entirely off; as Marines from another squad, the Hardass Squad, went out to retrieve him, they too were shot, "one at a time" (Hasford 108). Shortround restrained the Lusthog Marines from trying a rescue, even slugging Animal Mother in the face, and the sniper, after toying with the wounded men, finally dispatched them all (109). The second sniper works his mayhem in the jungle, wounding Alice, the prototype for Eightball, again and again, then doing the same to the rescue-minded Doc Jay (166–171). Now another Marine, known as the New Guy, makes a wild dash into the fray and gets shot in the throat (172). Cowboy manages to perform mercy killings on all three wounded men, but, in the process, gets shot several times himself (176). In a wrenching moment, Joker puts a bullet through Cowboy's left eye, and, as new squad leader, orders a retreat (178). By integrating the two episodes, Kubrick achieves compression and thus saves time, actually diminishes the level of violence, and dodges the redundancy of having one withering sniper attack followed by another.

Some of the smaller adaptive refinements also merit discussion.

Although he tends to lessen violence, Kubrick sometimes presents it with rhetorical flair. Here, Eightball's final agonies are delivered in slow motion.

Kubrick seems to have used the confrontation to create in microcosm a picture of America's troubles in the war as a whole. At the outset, the squad is lost (as it never is in the novel). When tensions and casualties rise, the Marines become torn by dissension. Their leader, Cowboy, is consumed with doubt, but tries, not too convincingly, to appear decisive in front of the men; in the end, he is swept along to disaster by an extraneous and irrational momentum. Indeed, switching the point of view so that suddenly we are sighting down the sniper's AK-47 jars and confuses us—which side are we on? Are the Marines our allies or our targets? The symbolic nature of the clash, hinted at in the source, is given fuller play by Kubrick, causing us to wonder at how and why this war was conducted. Very faintly, the film moralizes. It also appeals to pathos in a way that the hard-shelled novel scrupulously avoids. The fictional Joker's description of the war's deadly activities is cold and clinical:

Treated with callous humor in the novel, Cowboy's death is searingly tragic on screen.

> Doc Jay is on his feet and running. He runs at a crouch, zigzagging.
> *Bang.*
> Doc Jay stumbles, falls.
> The Doc's left thigh has been torn open. Jagged bone protrudes. The Doc tries to push himself forward with his good leg [Hasford 170].

But in the film, blood erupts from the men in vivid color; they collapse and roll in tortured slow motion; their agonized groans are prolonged. We are meant to sense their suffering and to feel unnerved by the ugly events that could cause such suffering. The manner of the film Cowboy's death likewise rakes at our sympathies, while bolstering our respectful image of Joker. In the novel, Joker shoots Cowboy in the head, and then, true to his callous code, jests about it: "Man-oh-man, Cowboy looks like a bag of leftovers from a V.F.W. barbecue" (178–79). How infinitely more stirring (and salable) it is to have Cowboy die in Joker's helpless arms; it is the sort of existential shock that Wilfred Owen converted to bitter poetry.

Led by Animal Mother, the Marines vow to "go get some payback." A smokescreen veils their movements, and they craftily penetrate the broken building that hides the sniper. Split off from the others, Joker enters a large, smoky room, lit by the licking flames of a recent attack. He peers around a column, sees the sniper standing at a window, and attempts to open fire on the figure—but his rifle jams. The sniper, whom we now see is a young Vietnamese girl, whirls and squeezes off several rounds at him, missing. Suddenly, her slim body is ripped by automatic fire: Rafterman, having trailed Joker into the room, has saved his life. With some curiosity the men congregate around the girl and watch her death throes. She prays in Vietnamese, and, in English, begs to be shot. Animal would prefer to leave her for the "mother-loving rats," but Joker quietly protests. When Animal gives him the option of executing her, Joker pauses, stares down at her, and shoots her. Impressed, Donlon calls him "hard-core."

The film's disposition of this emotional peak in the narrative differs rhetorically from the novel's along three major axes. First, Kubrick's handling of the initial confrontation is immensely more dramatic. In the novel, Joker, who has fallen stunned on his back, sees the (Hue) sniper only after she pins him with her foot (Hasford 116). His rifle does not jam, and, in fact, does not figure in the action whatever. She fires no shots at him—she understands that he is not a threat—and instead focuses on Rafterman, raising her SKS carbine at him just before he riddles her (116–17). By comparison, the film enlivens the scene, pouring into it as much surprise, fear, excitement, and catharsis as possible. Second, even though the film is more dramatic, it is less violent, less gruesome. Originally, the sniper's wounds are frightful: "Guts that look like colorful plastic have squirted out through bullet holes. The back of [her] right leg and her right buttock have been torn off" (118). After she dies, Animal Mother chops off her head; Rafterman fires a "long burst" from his M-16 into her body; and Alice chops off her feet and one of her fingers (120–21). By taming this aspect of the scene, Kubrick upgrades the collective character of the men, and stays within the bounds of an R rating. Finally, he makes separate, specific improvements to the persona of Joker. No longer does Joker call the sniper a "gook" as he does in the novel (116; 119). No longer does he answer harshly when asked: "What's she saying?" "What difference does it make?" the fictional Joker snaps (119). No longer does his mercy killing seem matter-of-fact: in the film, he must steel himself to commit the act, and we glimpse his internal struggle in the emotions that flicker across his face. The film Joker is someone with whom we are asked to relate.

Night has descended on Hue, which is now a blinding, crackling inferno. Joker, in voice-over, discloses that the Marines are headed for the Perfume River, where they will camp. As they "hump" along, they break into a full-throated rendition of the Mickey Mouse theme song, and Joker's thoughts drift toward erotic fantasy. He tells us he is happy to be "alive, in one piece, and short." He adds that while he may be in a "world of shit," he is not afraid. The shot dissolves into blackness, and white-lettered credits flash to the sounds of the Rolling Stones' "Paint It Black."

This final scene both omits pieces of the source, and discovers new uses for material that appears in the novel's middle section, "Body Count." At first glance, it may seem that Kubrick has dropped the novel's entire third and last section, "Grunts," in which the squad's reconnaissance of the jungle is terminated by the second sniper. But while the film's syuzhet does not encompass this action, the marrow of "Grunts" has hardly been lost; much of its language, tenor, and composition has been injected into the adaptive Vietnam segment, and especially into the Hue climax. Two items of note, however, have been excluded from the film: Rafterman's death, and Joker's eventual domination of Animal Mother. In the novel, following the combat in Hue, Rafterman gets run over—crushed—by an American tank (Hasford 129); the incident would seem to be one of the author's many comments on the folly of earthly life. By allowing Rafterman to live, the film enables us to track his growth as a character and to reflect on how much more growth he has yet to undergo. Besides, given the film's structure, one is left to puzzle at where Rafterman's death could reasonably occur: before or during the central skirmish would preclude his rescue of Joker; after would result in anticlimax. As to the fictional Joker, by the novel's end, he has (having killed Cowboy) assumed control of the squad and cowed Animal: Joker has but to wave his hand, and Animal takes the point position (180). The film Joker, a milder character than his forebear, does not travel that far. His contest is not with the other Marines, or even with the war, but with himself; he must rise above his own innate meekness in order to survive and prosper. His story is therefore more archetypal. The ingredients that comprise the film's closing scene are extracted from the heart of the source. Originally, Joker's satisfaction at being alive, short, and unafraid fills him when he and Rafterman are riding in the tank to Hue (77). Later, before the attack on the Citadel, a Marine begins to sing: "M.I.C.... K.E.Y.... M.O.U.S.E...." (98). Both elements work splendidly at the film's conclusion; in a text crowded with ironies, the Marines' singing of a child's innocent song while Hue burns behind them may be the ne plus ultra.

Some of the critical reactions to *Full Metal Jacket* serve to foreground the dilemma of the adapter. Several reviewers berated Kubrick for what they perceived as his unjustified faithfulness to the source. Whereas Tom O'Brien and Richard Lacayo mourned the loss of Hartman (458; 14), O'Brien, David Denby, and John Simon all condemned the film's duplex design (458; 54; "Bullet" 52). Denby, in fact, called the work "bizarre, a failed experiment that makes one aware of how conventional other movies are—and of why those conventions are necessary" (54). Against these shrill complaints, Lacayo proceeded to scourge Kubrick for his independence. "In the book," the critic wrote, "things are horrifying and then some.... Why did Kubrick make the movie if he didn't want to follow through?" (14). In my judgment, Kubrick did follow through, preserving (and sometimes expanding or reorganizing) what he deemed essential and abjuring everything else. Respecting his source, an underwritten and unbelievable novel, he adapted it into a raw and yet beautifully measured film: a compelling rhetorical emblem of a troubled time.

Chapter 5
Conclusions

In my analysis of three Stanley Kubrick films and the novels that spawned them, I have concerned myself chiefly with change: with how the original narrative evolves as it traverses the gap from one medium to the next. This focus is only logical, since change is at the center of the adaptive problem. If, hypothetically, source narratives never changed in being adapted, or changed in just nugatory ways, the transition could hardly be held problematic. Yet one must recognize that adaptation, at least with regard to the examples under study, involves a certain constancy as well; all is not, to borrow Yeats' phrase, "changed utterly."

One year before Kubrick directed *Fear and Desire*, his first commercial film, Lester Asheim observed that most adaptations embrace a broad fidelity to the source. Asheim found that the action comprising the "main plot line" of the novel is usually retained by the film ("usually" meaning in 80 percent of the cases he examined), and that the leading characters, while often simplified, typically adhere to the novelist's conception ("Summary" 269–70). These observations do not seem inapt in conjunction with the work of Kubrick. To cite just a single instance, one appreciates that Stephen King's *The Shining* deals with a would-be writer named Jack Torrance, his wife Wendy, and their gifted little boy Danny. The three spend part of a Colorado winter in a haunted hotel known as the Overlook. Jack goes berserk and, abetted by ghosts, tries to kill his family. In the end, Wendy and Danny escape, and Jack dies. Kubrick's film is faithful to every one of these generalities; more, it maintains the novel's horrifying tone, and features much of its language. Though one might take such basic and hyperopic fidelity for granted, it is not, as radical Donald Larsson has reminded us, a given (77). Insofar as one views adaptation from a distance, then, it may seem that the old adage *"Plus ça change, plus c'est la même chose"* is valid.

At the level of detail, however, adaptive changes in the rhetoric tend, as I have shown, to proliferate. Several of the changes occur with some consistency, and, even across my sample of three pairs of films and novels, inchoate patterns begin to emerge. I would like now to summarize the most prominent of these patterned changes, with the underlying thought that their recurrence is a key to understanding Kubrick's style both as a filmmaker and an adapter. Taken together, my core comments, which I have italicized below, form a kind of manual for Kubrickian adaptation.

1. *Regardless of how a novel may begin, Kubrick launches his adaptation of it with a heavily visual sequence that immediately and purposefully seizes our attention.* Chapter 1 of Nabokov's *Lolita* is a sunburst of the author's most rarefied prose (11), but that prose is tied to no particular action, and therefore would not translate happily to the screen. Kubrick counters this difficulty by opening with a sustained, close shot of Humbert's meticulously painting Lolita's toenails. No words are spoken, but the images, the movements, speak for themselves, and the film's guiding precept of obsessive love is promptly and convincingly set. King's *The Shining* begins in the midst of a jousting, but not terribly ominous, job interview (3–10); Kubrick opts to follow Jack from above on his way *to* the interview, the camera soaring and swooping like some bird of prey, the soundtrack alive with unearthly noises. One would never guess that an unchallenged drive through the mountains on a clear day could be made to seem so awful. And Gustav Hasford's *The Short-Timers* gets under way wanly, distantly:

> The Marines are looking for a few good men....
>   The recruit says that his name is Leonard Pratt.
>   Gunnery Sergeant Gerheim takes one look at the skinny redneck and immediately dubs him "Gomer Pyle" [3].

In his version, Kubrick shows us close-ups of the recruits enduring the rite of head-shaving; the scenes have a gelid quality that properly chills us and sets up the sergeant as a natural continuation. Kubrick wastes no time (and no words) in seeking not just to hook us, but to push us in a direction of his choosing.

    2. *Where it suits his purpose, Kubrick expunges parts of the original, including some characters, episodes, and swatches of dialog.* Those characters that he leaves behind are invariably minor (though one must bear in mind that they were, and are, important enough for the novelist to have included them in his matrix). Gone from Kubrick's *Lolita* are, among others, Annabel Leigh, Valeria, Gaston Godin, Mona Dahl, Headmistress Pratt, and Rita; from *The Shining,* Al Shockley, George Hatfield, and Jack's father; and from *Full Metal Jacket*, Privates Barnard and Perkins, Major Lynch, and General Motors. Other characters, though still present, are diminished in size and impact; some of these are Stuart Ullman, Bill Watson, Harry Derwent, and Roger in *The Shining*, and Captain January (reduced to a mention) in *Full Metal Jacket*. The loss of such characters and their attendant activities tightens the narrative's structure and gooses its pace; it may also—as with Al Shockley and George Hatfield—simplify the story, or—as with Gaston Godin— give it a different tincture. Sometimes a character who survives may assume some of the duties of one who has not: Charlotte plays chess in lieu of Gaston; Lieutenant Lockhart, a new character, stands in largely for Major Lynch, but also seems to have absorbed some of Captain January's air of blasé corruptness.

    All sorts of episodes are omitted, ranging from the very large to the very small. Each film dispenses with a few of the former and a bevy of the latter. Among the more formidable blocks of material excised are, from *Lolita*, Humbert's early life in Europe, his and Lolita's first *Wanderjahr* across America, his attempt to piece together the literary clues left by Quilty, and his two-year travels with Rita. From *The Shining*, Kubrick excludes most of the tedious background information on the Torrances, Jack's misdoings with the wasps' nest, and of course the hedge animals. From *Full Metal Jacket*, he drops Joker's sojourn in Phu Bai, and the capping patrol through the jungle (although the essence of the patrol is, in the film, blended into another adventure). One notices that most of these episodes, while adding to the plot, do not propel the narrative to its next level of development; they are, with the exception of the catastrophic patrol, quite static. Like the larger omissions, the smaller ones serve to speed the story, though now we more regularly encounter the collateral effects of modifying a character or leavening the film's tone. In the novel, Humbert makes repeated visits to a mental hospital; in the film, he does not—hence, the adaptive Humbert is rendered more wholesome. In the novel, Danny finds a clock whose paired figurines perform oral sex on each other; in the film, he makes no such discovery—the adaptive narrative is made more roundly acceptable. In the novel, Rafterman eats a piece of human flesh; in the film, he does not—both the adaptive character and the film are guided toward the mainstream of everyday values.

When characters and episodes are eliminated, it follows that most, though not necessarily all, of their dialog will vanish with them. But often, Kubrick keeps the characters and much of what they do, and yet still reduces the number of words spoken. In terms of language expended, he understands that one of the qualities most cherished by all screenwriters is "economy" (Wald 65–66). My analyses contain several illustrations of Kubrick's relative parsimony with dialog, and I will provide one more herewith. Although *The Short-Timers* is nothing if not concise, even many of its exchanges have been slashed for the screen. Compare the following parallel passages, the first from the novel:

> Fuck freedom. Flush out your headgear, New Guy. You think we waste gooks for *free*dom? Don't kid yourself; this is a slaughter. You've got to open your eyes, New Guy—you owe it to yourself. If I'm gonna get *my* balls shot off for a word I get to pick my own word and my word is *poontang*. Yeah, you better believe we zap zipperheads. They waste our bros [*sic*] and we cut them a big piece of payback. And payback is a motherfucker [Hasford 159].

In the film, this speech, uttered by Animal Mother, is contracted to:

> Flush out your headgear, New Guy. You think we waste gooks for freedom? This is a slaughter. If I'm gonna get my balls blown off for a word, my word is "poontang."

In all, Kubrick would seem to agree with Lionel Godfrey, who postulated that, with a screenplay, "what is omitted is often more important than what is put in" (12).

3. *Addressing himself to the portion of the narrative that remains, Kubrick distorts, reorders, and conflates many of its components.* An explicit case of distortion is Lolita's robust physical appearance in the film, as against her waiflike nature in the novel. By presenting the girl as more mature, and more breathtakingly attractive, Kubrick steers his project away from the shoals of pedophilia and toward the more navigable waters of a healthy, if ill-advised, romantic attachment. An instance of reordering occurs in *The Shining* when Kubrick juggles the events that make up the Torrances' introduction to the Overlook. Unlike the novel, the film accords Dick the final word before the staff departs; that final word is a cautionary one—stay away from Room 237, he warns Danny—and puts us on edge in a way that the book does not. A patent example conflation appears in *Full Metal Jacket,* as Joker views a mass grave, and then must fend off a loutish Colonel. In the source, these events are entirely separate. Yoking them together effectuates narrational compaction, and also ennobles Joker, who seems large-minded in the company of his interrogator, a man more concerned with Joker's peace button than with 20 dead civilians. At times, one encounters all three operations—distortion, reordering, and conflation—simultaneously, in the transposition of dialog from one character or situation to another; this maneuver is common to *Full Metal Jacket.*

4. *Although skilled with words, Kubrick is equally skilled with and devoted to images, and he tells his stories as visually as possible.* This tendency, which is a hallmark of every extraordinary director, relates to Kubrick's penchant for cutting dialog, and to his habitual search for objective correlatives; it also relates to his knack for discovering compelling shots simply to bewitch the eye. In *Lolita,* Humbert's lust is suggested by his voracious bite of a dangling fried egg; his desire to murder his wife is inscribed in the sullen stare he locks on a pistol. His fumbling with the cot insinuates his, and the film's, skittishness about his pending intimacy with Lolita, and the bulletholes through Quilty's painting comment sadly on the heroine's ruined life. In *The Shining,* Wendy's tensions may be seen in her

ever-present cigarette, held in a hand that sometimes trembles. Tony is reified from Danny's internal impression into his waggly, "talking" finger. Deep-focus shots communicate the cavelike dimensions of the hotel, and tracking shots of Danny on his tricycle provoke our anxiety. What Jack experiences in Room 237 is strongly visual, not verbal, and all the more eerie because of it. In *Full Metal Jacket*, we see Pyle's early incompetence, then see his improvement, then see finally the madness that alters him physically. Rafterman's nausea on the helicopter bespeaks his emotional turmoil, as do his shaking hands during the battle. The three-man camera crew that creeps backward along the ragged fringe of Hue delights us with its unnatural movement, and the poppling flames that scorch the wreckage appall us. Kubrick betrays no undue hostility toward words, and frequently revels in them, but the reverence that this one-time still photographer has for visuality is undeniable.

    5. *In general, Kubrick lowers the amount and intensity of violence found in the original.* Nabokov's *Lolita,* more debated for its psychosexual deviance than for any exceptional violence, nonetheless does have its moments of graphic physical roughness and even destructiveness. If the film Charlotte's condition after she is struck by a car seems not far removed from a sound sleep, we get no such illusion in the novel: the top of her head is a "porridge of bone, brains, bronze hair, and blood" (*Lolita* 100). Outwardly a genteel fellow in the film, Humbert proves himself a ruffian in the source. Half-crazed with jealousy and paranoia during his second cross-country flight with Lolita, he pushes her into a room and wildly strip-searches her, hoping to find some vague clue that would establish her infidelity (217). Later, he hits her in the face (229). As in the film, Humbert reserves his greatest violence for Quilty, whom he murders. But in the book, the episode is longer, gaudier, and more grotesque. The adaptive Quilty's death is comparatively hygienic—no blood, minimal suffering—and we do not see the quietus: the victim huddles behind a large portrait, dying in privacy.

    A similar diminution is evidenced across the two versions of *The Shining.* In the novel, Jack is guilty of *breaking* Danny's arm, not of dislocating his shoulder (*Shining* 17). We read of Jack's assault on George Hatfield—"Jack [wades] in, his fists held up in front of him" (115)—and of the dream-George's attempt to strangle Jack (271–72). Having escaped from the pantry, Jack batters Wendy with a mallet, and she answers by stabbing him deeply with a knife (396–97). When he finally corners Danny, Jack, or what shell remains of him, begins hammering himself in the face with the mallet: "Blood splatter[s] across the wallpaper. Shards of bone [leap] into the air like broken piano keys. It is impossible to say just how long it [goes] on" (429). Entering Jack's memories, we witness his burly father's beating Jack's mother with a gold-knobbed cane, bashing her to the floor during a Sunday dinner (224-25). And unlike the film, the novel does have the hag in Room 217 close her hands on Danny's throat (218). In only one instance is the film more violent than the original, that being the ax murder of Dick. By and large, the adaptive tide clearly flows in the opposite direction.

More than the other films, *Full Metal Jacket* is characterized by violence, but its savagery, even so, is an abridgment and an etiolation of what happens in the source. Rather than choke Pyle for his impertinent smile as Hartman does, Gerheim hits him repeatedly (Hasford 6). Indeed, beatings are a "routine element of life on Parris Island.... Gerheim and his three junior drill instructors administer brutal beatings to faces, chests, stomachs, and backs. With fists. Or boots ..." (7). During bayonet training, Gerheim drives a rifle butt into Private Barnard's mouth, breaking loose two of his teeth; Barnard skewers the sergeant's right thigh with a bayonet; Gerheim ends the matter by knocking the private unconscious (14–15). On another occasion, Gerheim crams Pyle's head into a toilet's "yellow pool. [Pyle] struggles. Bubbles. Panic gives [Pyle] strength; Sergeant Gerheim holds him down" (16). In Vietnam, a tank containing Joker and Rafterman mashes a tiny girl (78), and Rafterman too ultimately gets severed in half by a tank (129). Animal Mother is a dedicated rapist (90–91); Alice carries a bag full of "foul-smelling gook feet" (149), and Joker uses his rifle to threaten an MP (54), his knife to threaten Animal (162–63), and then calmly puts a bullet through Cowboy's brain (178). All these fictional acts and suggestions of violence Kubrick has either subdued or kept from his film totally, victims of his aesthetic or, perhaps, his pragmatism in the face of the Motion Picture Association of America.

6. *As Kubrick remakes the original narrative, he tends, with some exceptions, to simplify it.* Overall, in adapting a novel, he subtracts more material than he adds; the length of the story is therefore shortened, but so is its complexity reduced. In Kubrick's *Lolita*, Humbert consorts with no females besides Charlotte and her daughter. But the fictional Humbert spends time also with Annabel, with prostitutes, with Valeria, and with Rita; the novel thus invites us to take a more seasoned and liberal view of his tastes and values in women. Kubrick's *The Shining* shadows forth the notion that Jack goes murderously insane due to the baleful influence of the haunted hotel. The novel certainly includes this plot strain, but it also portrays Jack as a complicated, frustrated man at odds with himself and his world; the etiology of his sickness is less pat. In *Full Metal Jacket*, we witness the death of Touchdown, and we know that Animal Mother is not responsible. But in the novel, Animal and others drop hints that he has murdered the lieutenant by "fragging" him. By omitting this wrinkle, the film manages not to raise a series of rhetorical questions that could derail the narrative's momentum: If Animal kills the lieutenant, what is his motivation? Is his action justified? What do the other men think of it? If he does not kill the lieutenant, why does he let on that he has? Again, the arc of the film's story is cleaner and plainer than the novel's. As I mentioned, one may notice some exceptions to this adaptive bent, such as Kubrick's vexatious shot of Wendy and Danny in the miniature maze, and the 1921 photograph of Jack that hangs on the Overlook's wall. But items that actually augment the source's complexity are made conspicuous by their rarity.

7. *Kubrick makes his heroes more virtuous than the novels' and his villains more wicked.* This adjustment may also be seen as a form of simplification, since many of the characters' contradictory impurities are washed away. Humbert's image is enhanced by what he does and does not do, and by the image shift of those around him. In the film, he is taken with Lolita romantically and not just libidinously (as witness the pedicure); he is willing to confront overwhelming forces, such as Dr. Keegy and the staff at the hospital, to keep her; and, in the end, he bestows on her a more exorbitant sum of money. Conversely, the adaptive Humbert does not, so far as we can tell,

have a tainted past; he does not furtively grope at Lolita; he does not plan to drug her; he never strikes her; and he is not seen with a variety of women. Moreover, he is surrounded by others whose sexual hunger apparently exceeds his own: Charlotte, John and Jean, Miss Starch. In *Full Metal Jacket,* Joker benefits from a like transformation. The film Joker is warmer and more sensitive than the original, as we observe in his treatment of Pyle, his grief at the graveside, his aching hesitancy at carrying out the sniper's execution. At the same time, a skein of omissions operates on his behalf. He no longer supposes that death is his friend, or that "God has a hard-on for Marines" (Hasford 47; 150); nor does he concoct an atrocity photograph or kiss a dead rat. Above all, he does not kill Cowboy, an act whose kindly intention is draped in moral ambiguity. Like Humbert, Joker has been reimagined as a decent if ordinary man who happens to find himself enmeshed in trying circumstances.

Kubrick's villains likewise become less variegated, more extreme in their villainy. In Nabokov's *Lolita,* Humbert's criminality is given unclouded recognition—throughout the text, he fancies himself as addressing a jury—while Quilty is a faint and Puckish presence who is barely noticeable until the novel is nearly concluded. In the film, with Humbert something of a romantic and tragic hero, Quilty's role is expanded and darkened, so that he is now clearly the locus of evil. The demonic company of his black-edged lady friend seems to suit him, as does the fellowship, not seen in the source, of the loathsome hotelier Swine. The adaptive Quilty's verbal ambush of Humbert on the veranda amounts to browbeating, and in assuming the admonitory function of Headmistress Pratt, he connives openly, as Dr. Zempf, to possess Lolita. His late-night call to the sickly Humbert, which does not occur in the book, is mere cruelty. Jack Torrance's place in *The Shining,* though not much expanded—it is already large—is also clarified to his detriment. The film Jack performs acts that the fictional Jack does not: at the start, he delights in telling Danny about cannibalism; further along, he consciously disables the CB radio; in the end, he murders Dick. As much as these commissions change his persona, a nexus of omissions affects it even more. We no longer see the effort it costs him not to drink; we receive no sense that he may be a writer of some ability and ambition; we notice no productivity in him at all (his typing is revealed as a sham); and we miss his eleventh hour expression of love for his son.

   8. *Predominately, Kubrick imbues his films with a morality that is more conventional than the novels'.* Much of this effect is achieved through the purification of the heroes and villains: good is good; evil is evil; and we are freed, to a greater extent than in the book, from sorting through any bothersome subtleties. Other adaptive steps, too, restrain and normalize the films' moral drift. The eroticism of the original *Lolita* is shrunk to little more than a sprinkle of salacious patter, and Humbert's attraction to the girl seems less a product of testosterone than of quixotic love. This possibility, coupled with Lolita's unspecified age and her womanly appearance, somewhat extenuates Humbert's sexual indiscretions. Regardless, the text signals us when he first teeters on the brink of impropriety, and implicitly it asks our disapproval: we are given Quilty as police officer, and nervous, slapstick comedy with the cot. The case of *The Shining* is less clear-cut. By simplifying both the plot and Jack's character, the film presents a story in which the protagonist-villain quickly goes insane and attacks his loving family. No palliating conditions apply, and we are thus invited to root wholeheartedly against Jack. Offsetting this moral clarity, however, is the death of Dick, who perhaps deserves, and in the novel receives, a mellower fate. But the trend reasserts itself vigorously in *Full Metal Jacket*, with its reduction in violence, its elimination of atrocity, and its blanket refurbishment of the Marines' habits, values, and style. A barbaric figure in the novel, Joker in particular has been transfigured into a moral leader, a warrior whose abiding emotions are resolve and regret, not excitement and anger. In fact, the film gives a literalness to the hoary chestnut attributed to William Tecumseh Sherman: the flames of Hue proclaim again that war is hell.

   9. *Kubrick's films are more obviously laced with moments of moderate-to-high drama than are the source materials.* Part of this tendency owes to his practice of decreasing dialog while increasing visuality (which often equates with action). Put simply, since the characters are saying less and doing more, opportunities for a dramatic

flourish naturally occur at shorter intervals. But the films' exclamation points do not usually result simply from dropping some verbiage here or adding a visual fillip there; rather, they are inserted by rewriting and restaging relatively low-key fictional moments to bring them more zest and more meaning. A development that the first author has handled routinely now becomes a matter of some reckoning. Each of the three films abounds with incidents that are captured more broadly, bluntly, and emphatically than in the original. From *Lolita* one recalls Humbert's initial, sun-blessed view of the nymphet, his final kiss on her cheek, his humiliating scuffle in the hospital, his awkward reunion with Lolita in Coalmont. From *The Shining* one remembers the doctor's frown at hearing of Jack's violence, Jack's direful visit to Room 237, Wendy's alarming discovery about his writing, Jack's gimlet discussion with Grady in the restroom. From *Full Metal Jacket* one recollects Hartman's demand to see Joker's "war face," the late-night debacle with Pyle in the latrine, Lockhart's banishment of Joker to Phu Bai, Joker's near-disastrous encounter with the sniper. For inclusion in the adaptation, each of these moments has been shrewdly structured or restructured so as to milk our emotions; just as we are asked to think, we are asked now, more than before, to feel.

  10. *From time to time, though it countervails his mainly reductive thrust, Kubrick expands one or more aspects of the original narrative.* I have noted that Quilty has been enlarged for the screen. Indeed, so tenuous is his presence in the novel that Nabokovian scholar Carl Proffer has devoted one full chapter of his *Keys to* Lolita to tracking the playwright's ghostly movements through the source (55–78). No such guide is needed for the film. Sergeant Gerheim's role likewise swells when he becomes Sergeant Hartman. Though I would not place Gerheim/Hartman in the same villainous class as Quilty, David Denby might disagree:

> Hartman isn't secretly benevolent. He brutalizes the men because he wants to turn out killers for the Marine Corps—and because he enjoys it. Happily malevolent, he's an inspired and profane ideologue of war, controlling his men, then releasing them to kill and die. In the end, he is not their protector and friend but their executioner [54].

So one must understand that a villain, or an adversary, may be given a wider scope in an adaptation; this manipulation is likely to produce more personal conflict, and more drama. Elements of the narrative other than characters may also be accorded increased prominence. In *Lolita*, whereas sexual activity is erased, sexual innuendo is multiplied; in *Full Metal Jacket*, whereas violence is diminished, violent language, especially from Hartman, is intensified. In these special instances, one senses a compensation that does not ordinarily obtain in the world of adaptation: words have been substituted for actions. Sometimes an image may be more richly developed, as with Grady's unfortunate daughters in *The Shining*, or a segment of the narrative may be given fuller treatment, as with the Parris Island stave of *Full Metal Jacket*. Kubrick reserves the right to adjust a narrative's proportions to accommodate his taste and vision.

11. *Now and then, Kubrick invents his own material outright, and imposes it on the new narrative.* In so doing, he seems to be pursuing one of two aims, or conceivably both. First, he may be attempting to tighten or shore up a design that, left alone, would falter in the film medium. Examples of this response include the dance sequence in *Lolita*, which elegantly saves time by drawing together several major characters at once, and the theater scene in *Full Metal Jacket*, which extends the Marines' respite between battles, thereby improving the story's rhythm. Second, he may be seeking to press his own stylistic cachet upon the film's rhetoric. Examples here include the interjection of the unknown girl's portrait in *Lolita* and the suggestion in *The Shining* that Jack is atavistically acquainted with the Overlook. As with Kubrick's occasional expansion of items in the source, his incorporation of wholly new matter into the fabula is done both selectively and infrequently.

Although celebrated and chided as an idiosyncratic artist, Stanley Kubrick has demonstrated within his own projects a definite consistency of adaptive technique. Moreover, his basic approach to adaptation is not, by the evidence, hugely different from that employed by legions of others who have turned novels into films. Comparing the two media, André Bazin stressed the value of finding cinematic equivalents for literary artifices (68); Alice Field cited the need to keep a film's moral tone in line with the vaunted

Production Code (50); DeWitt Bodeen noted film's bias toward drama (355–56); Donald McCaffrey wrote of the adapter's obligation to compress (14–17); Bernard Dick maintained that cinema lifts the visual over the verbal (73–74). Each of these discernments, while not directed at Kubrick, resonates agreeably when applied to his films. So from this standpoint, one is brought not just to acknowledge the trends that emerge within Kubrick's work, but to realize that they seem loosely to prevail across the wide expanse of commercial adaptation. As an adapter, Kubrick must be viewed as part of a rhetorical community.

But despite this grand framework that unites most if not all adapters, Kubrick's films are unique and personal. They achieve their rhetorical identity only after the implementation of untold decisions involving, among other variables, what to drop, what to keep, and what to change. These decisions are not arrived at without the expenditure of time, labor, and judicious thought, for the alterations and constancies are multileveled and interdependent. They present themselves several at a time, and fit inside each other like so many Chinese boxes. As such, adaptation has less to do with Richard Corliss' notion of surgery and silicone ("Wrong Arm" 58) than with what Vladimir Nabokov saw as the "refuge of art" (*Lolita* 311).

Bibliography

Allen, Walter. "Simply Lolita." Rev. of *Lolita*, by Vladimir Nabokov. *New Statesman* 7 Nov. 1959: 631–32.
Alpert, Hollis. "The Bubble Gum Siren." Rev. of *Lolita*. *Saturday Review* 23 June 1962: 40.
Andrew, Dudley. *Concepts in Film Theory*. Oxford: Oxford University Press, 1984.
Andrews, James R. *The Practice of Rhetorical Criticism*. New York: Macmillan Publishing Company, 1983.
Appel, Alfred, Jr., ed. *The Annotated Lolita*. By Vladimir Nabokov. New York: McGraw-Hill Book Company, 1970.
Aristotle. *Rhetoric*. Trans. W. Rhys Roberts. *The Rhetoric and Poetics of Aristotle*. New York: The Modern Library, 1954.
Asheim, Lester. "From Book to Film: Mass Appeals." *Hollywood Quarterly* 5 (1951): 334–49.
———. "From Book to Film: The Note of Affirmation." *The Quarterly of Film, Radio, and Television* 6 (1952): 54–68.
———. "From Book to Film: Simplification." *Hollywood Quarterly* 5 (1951): 289–304.
———. "From Book to Film: Summary." *The Quarterly of Film, Radio, and Television* 6 (1952): 258–73.
Ball, John. Rev. of *The Shining*, by Stephen King. *BooksWest* Oct. 1977: 21.
Bannon, Barbara A. Rev. of *The Shining*, by Stephen King. *Publishers Weekly* 6 Dec. 1976: 52.
Barthes, Roland. *S/Z*. Trans. Richard Miller. New York: Hill and Wang, 1974.
Baskin, Ellen, and Mandy Hicken. *Enser's Filmed Books and Plays*. Brookfield, VT: Ashgate Publishing Company, 1993.
Bauer, Leda. "The Movies Tackle Literature." *American Mercury* July 1928: 288–94.
Bazin, André. "In Defense of Mixed Cinema." *What Is Cinema?* Ed. and trans. Hugh Gray. Vol. 1. Berkeley: University of California Press, 1967. 53–75. 2 vols.

Beahm, George, ed. *The Stephen King Companion*. Kansas City, MS: Andrews and McMeel, 1989.
Beatty, Jack. Rev. of *The Short-Timers*, by Gustav Hasford. *New Republic* 27 Jan. 1979: 39–40.
Beckley, Paul V. "Lolita." Rev. of *Lolita*. *New York Herald Tribune* 14 June 1962: 16.
Beja, Morris. *Film and Literature*. New York: Longman, Inc., 1979.
Benson, Thomas W., and Carolyn Anderson. *Reality Fictions: The Films of Frederick Wiseman*. Carbondale, IL: Southern Illinois University Press, 1989.
Bernstein, Jeremy. "How About a Little Game?" *New Yorker* 12 Nov. 1966: 70+.
Block, Maxine. "Films Adapted from Published Works." *Wilson Library Bulletin* Feb. 1936: 394–97.
Bluestone, George. *Novels into Film*. Berkeley: University of California Press, 1957.
Bodeen, DeWitt. "The Adapting Art." *Films in Review* 14 (1963): 349–56.
Booth, Wayne C. *The Rhetoric of Fiction*. Chicago: The University of Chicago Press, 1961.
Bordwell, David. *Making Meaning: Inference and Rhetoric in the Interpretation of Cinema*. Cambridge: Harvard University Press, 1989.
Brenner, Conrad. "Nabokov: The Art of the Perverse." *New Republic* 23 June 1958: 18–21.
Brock, Bernard L., Robert L. Scott, and James W. Chesebro, eds. *Methods of Rhetorical Criticism: A Twentieth-Century Perspective*. 3rd ed. Detroit: Wayne State University Press, 1989.
Bromell, Henry. "The Dimming of Stanley Kubrick." Rev. of *The Shining*. *Atlantic Monthly* Aug. 1980: 80–83.
Brooks, Cleanth, and Robert Penn Warren. *Understanding Poetry*. 3rd ed. New York: Holt, Rinehart and Winston, 1960.
Bryant, Donald C. *Rhetorical Dimensions in Criticism*. Baton Rouge: Louisiana State University Press, 1973.
Bunzel, Peter. "Yes, They Did It: *Lolita Is* a Movie." *Life* 25 May 1962: 93–97.
Butcher, Maryvonne. "Look First upon this Picture: Books and Films." *Wiseman Review* 238 (1964): 55–64.
Bywater, Tim, and Thomas Sobchack. *An Introduction to Film Criticism: Major Critical Approaches to Narrative Film*. New York: Longman Inc., 1989.
Clemons, Walter. "Killing Ground." Rev. of *The Short-Timers*, by Gustav Hasford. *Newsweek* 1 Jan. 1979: 60.
Conaty, Barbara. Rev. of *The Shining*, by Stephen King. *Library Journal* 1 Feb. 1977: 404.

Corliss, Richard. "Welcome to Viet Nam, the Movie: II." Rev. of *Full Metal Jacket. Time* 29 June 1987: 66.

———. "The Wrong Arm of the Law." *Time* 5 July 1993: 58.

Crowther, Bosley. "Screen: *Lolita,* Vladimir Nabokov's Adaptation of His Novel." Rev. of *Lolita. New York Times* 14 June 1962: 23.

Curran, Ronald T. "Complex, Archetype, and Primal Fear: King's Use of Fairy Tales in *The Shining." The Dark Descent: Essays Defining Stephen King's Horrorscape.* Ed. Tony Magistrale. New York: Greenwood Press, 1992. 33–46.

Curtis, Francis H. Rev. of *The Short-Timers,* by Gustav Hasford. *Best Sellers* June 1979: 77.

Davies, Robert A., James M. Farrell, and Steven S. Matthews. "The Dream World of Film: A Jungian Perspective on Cinematic Communication." *Western Journal of Speech Communication* 46 (1982): 326–43.

Denby, David. "Death Trap." Rev. of *Full Metal Jacket. New York* 13 July 1987: 54.

Dick, Bernard F. "Authors, Auteurs, and Adaptations: Literature As Film / Film As Literature." *Yearbook of American Comparative and General Literature* 27 (1978): 72–76.

"Domestic Box Office." *Variety* 27 Dec. 1993: 24.

Duffy, Martha, and Richard Schickel. "Kubrick's Grandest Gamble." *Time* 15 Dec. 1975: 72–78.

Durgnat, Raymond. "Lolita." Rev. of *Lolita. Films and Filming* Nov. 1962: 35.

Dwan, Allan. "Filming Great Fiction: Can Literature Be Preserved in Motion Pictures?" *The Forum* 62 (1919): 298–305.

Eberwein, Robert T. *A Viewer's Guide to Film Theory and Criticism.* Metuchen, NJ: The Scarecrow Press, Inc., 1979.

Eidsvik, Charles. "Toward a *'Politique des Adaptations.'*" *Literature/Film Quarterly* 3 (1975): 255–63.

Eliot, T. S. "Hamlet and His Problems." *The Sacred Wood: Essays on Poetry and Criticism.* New York: Barnes & Noble, Inc., 1920. 95-103.

———. "The Three Voices of Poetry." *On Poetry and Poets.* London: Faber and Faber Limited, 1957. 89–102.

———. "Tradition and the Individual Talent." *The Sacred Wood: Essays on Poetry and Criticism.* New York: Barnes & Noble, Inc., 1920. 47–59.

Fadiman, William. "But Compared to the Original." *Films and Filming* Feb. 1965: 21–23.

———. "The New-Style Myth Makers." *Films and Filming* Aug. 1961: 30.

Field, Alice Evans. *Hollywood, U. S. A.: From Script to Screen.* New York: Vantage Press, 1952.

Foss, Sonja. *Rhetorical Criticism: Exploration and Practice.* Prospect Heights, IL: Waveland Press, 1989.

Freud, Sigmund. *Jokes and Their Relation to the Unconscious*. Ed. and trans. James Strachey. London: Routledge & Kegan Paul, 1960.

Full Metal Jacket. Dir. Stanley Kubrick. With Matthew Modine, Adam Baldwin, Vincent D'Onofrio, and Lee Ermey. Warner Bros., 1987.

Godfrey, Lionel. "It Wasn't Like That in the Book." *Films and Filming* Apr. 1967: 12–16.

Goldman, William. *Adventures in the Screen Trade: A Personal View of Hollywood and Screenwriting*. New York: Warner Books, 1983.

Golson, G. Barry, ed. *The* Playboy *Interview*. New York: Wideview Books, 1981.

Groves, Don. "O'seas B.O. Adds Up to Jolly Season." *Variety* 27 Dec. 1993: 26+.

Hart, Roderick. *Modern Rhetorical Criticism*. Glenview, IL: Scott, Foresman and Company, 1990.

Hartung, Phillip T. "Of Human Bondage." Rev. of *Lolita*. *Commonweal* 13 July 1962: 401–2.

Harvey, Stephen. "'Shining' It Isn't." *Saturday Review* July 1980: 64–65.

Hasford, Gustav. *The Short-Timers*. New York: Bantam Books, 1980.

Hatch, Robert. "Practice Makes Perfect." Rev. of *The Shining*. *Nation* 14 June 1980: 732.

Herr, Michael. Foreword. *Full Metal Jacket: The Screenplay*. By Stanley Kubrick, Michael Herr, and Gustav Hasford. New York: Alfred A. Knopf, 1987. v-vii.

Hicks, Granville. "*Lolita* and Her Problems." *Saturday Review* 16 Aug. 1958: 12+.

Horne, William Leonard. *"A Starting Point": A Critical Approach to the Role of the Screenplay in the Adaptation of Novels for the Cinema*. Diss. The University of Wisconsin-Madison, 1982. Ann Arbor: UMI, 1986. 83-04947.

Houston, Penelope. "Kubrick Country." *Saturday Review* 25 Dec. 1971: 42–44.

Hughes, Riley. "Lolita." Rev. of *Lolita*, by Vladimir Nabokov. *Catholic World* Oct. 1958: 72.

"Humbert Humdrum & Lullita." Rev. of *Lolita*. *Time* 22 June 1962: 94.

Huselberg, Richard A. "Novels and Films: A Limited Inquiry." *Literature/Film Quarterly* 6 (1978): 57–65.

Iser, Wolfgang. *The Implied Reader: Patterns of Communication in Prose Fiction from Bunyan to Beckett*. Baltimore: The Johns Hopkins University Press, 1974.

Jameson, Richard T. "Kubrick's Shining." Rev. of *The Shining*. *Film Comment* 16.4 (1980): 28–32.

Janeway, Elizabeth. "The Tragedy of Man Driven by Desire." Rev. of *Lolita*, by Vladimir Nabokov. *New York Times Book Review* 17 Aug. 1958: 5+.

Kael, Pauline. "Devolution." Rev. of *The Shining*. *New Yorker* 9 June 1980: 130–47.

———. "Ponderoso." Rev. of *Full Metal Jacket*. *New Yorker* 13 July 1987: 75–76.

Kagan, Norman. *The Cinema of Stanley Kubrick*. New York: Holt, Rinehart and Winston, 1972.

Kanfer, Stefan. "King of Horror." *The Shape under the Sheet: The Complete Stephen King Encyclopedia*. Ed. Stephen J. Spignesi. Ann Arbor: Popular Culture, 1991. 17-23.

Kauffmann, Stanley. "The Dulling." Rev. of *The Shining*. *New Republic* 14 June 1980: 26–27.

———. "Humbug Humbug." Rev. of *Lolita*. *New Republic* 2 July 1962: 29–30.

King, Stephen. *Danse Macabre*. New York: Everest House, 1981.

———. "The *Playboy* Interview." *The Stephen King Companion*. Ed. George Beahm. Kansas City, MS: Andrews and McMeel, 1989. 19–45.

———. *The Shining*. New York: Signet, 1978.

Kinney, Judy Lee. "Text and Pretext: Stanley Kubrick's Adaptations." Diss. University of California Los Angeles, 1982.

Kolker, Robert Phillip. *A Cinema of Loneliness*. 2nd ed. New York: Oxford University Press, 1988.

Kroll, Jack. "1968: Kubrick's Vietnam Odyssey." Rev. of *Full Metal Jacket*. *Newsweek* 29 June 1987: 64–65.

———. "Stanley Kubrick's Horror Show." Rev. of *The Shining*. *Newsweek* 26 May 1980: 96–99.

Kubrick, Stanley. "Words and Movies." *Hollywood Directors: 1941–1976*. Ed. Richard Koszarski. New York: Oxford University Press, 1977. 306–9.

Lacayo, Richard. "Semper Fi: Kubrick Sticks to His Guns." Rev. of *Full Metal Jacket*. *Film Comment* 23.5 (1987): 11–14.

Larsson, Donald F. "Novel into Film: Some Preliminary Reconsiderations." *Transformations in Literature and Film*. Ed. Leon Golden. Tallahassee: University Presses of Florida, 1982. 69–83.

Lehman, Peter, ed. *Close Viewings: An Anthology of New Film Criticism*. Tallahassee: The Florida State University Press, 1990.

Lingeman, Richard R. "Something Nasty in the Tub." Rev. of *The Shining*, by Stephen King. *New York Times* 1 Mar. 1977: 35.

Lolita. Dir. Stanley Kubrick. With James Mason, Shelley Winters, Peter Sellers, and Sue Lyon. MGM/UA, 1961.

"Lolita." Rev. of *Lolita*. *Variety* 13 June 1962: 6.

MacDonald, Dwight. "Of Nymphets and Monsterettes." Rev. of *Lolita*. *Esquire* Sept. 1962: 45–46.

Macgowan, Kenneth. *Behind the Screen: The History and Techniques of the Motion Picture*. New York: Delacorte Press, 1965.

Madsen, Roy Paul. *The Impact of Film: How Ideas Are Communicated Through Cinema and Television*. New York: Macmillan Publishing Company, 1973.
Martin, Wallace. *Recent Theories of Narration*. Ithaca: Cornell University Press, 1986.
Max, D. T. "What Makes a Book Hot in Hollywood?" *Elle* Sept. 1993: 128–32.
McCaffrey, Donald W. "Adaptation Problems of the Two Unique Media: The Novel and the Film." *The Dickinson Review* 1 (1967): 11–17.
McFarlane, Brian. *Words and Images: Australian Novels into Film*. Richmond, Victoria: Heinemann Publishers Australia, 1983.
Meyer, Frank S. "A Lance into Cotton Wool: The Strange Fate of *Lolita*." *National Review* 22 Nov. 1958: 340–41.
Mitry, Jean. "Remarks on the Problem of Adaptation." *Midwest Modern Language Association Bulletin* 12 (1971): 1–9.
Molnar, Thomas. "Matter-of-Fact Confession of a Non-Penitent." Rev. of *Lolita*, by Vladimir Nabokov. *Commonweal* 24 Oct. 1958: 102.
Nabokov, Vladimir. *Lolita*. Ed. Alfred Appel, Jr. New York: McGraw-Hill Book Company, 1970.
———. *Lolita: A Screenplay*. New York: McGraw-Hill Book Company, 1974.
———. "On a Book Entitled *Lolita*." *The Annotated* Lolita. By Nabokov. Ed. Alfred Appel, Jr. New York: McGraw-Hill Book Company, 1970. 313–19.
Nelson, Thomas Allen. *Kubrick: Inside a Film Artist's Maze*. Bloomington: Indiana University Press, 1982.
Niebuhr, Reinhold. Rev. of *Lolita*. *Show* Aug. 1962: 63–69.
O'Brien, Tom. "Satired Out." Rev. of *Full Metal Jacket*. *Commonweal* 14 Aug. 1987: 457–58.
Orwell, George. "Good Bad Books." *The Collected Essays, Journalism and Letters of George Orwell. In Front of Your Nose: 1945-1950*. Ed. Sonja Orwell and Ian Angus. New York: Harcourt, Brace & World, Inc., 1968. 19–22.
Phillips, Gene. "Kubrick." *Film Comment* 7.4 (1972): 30–35.
Poe, Edgar Allan. "Ulalume." *Selected Poetry and Prose of Poe*. Ed. T. O. Mabbott. New York: The Modern Library, 1951. 38–40.
Pope, Alexander. "An Essay On Criticism." *The Literature of England*. Ed. George K. Anderson and William E. Buckler. 5th ed. Glenview, IL: Scott, Foresman and Company, 1968. 1533–44.
Proffer, Carl R. *Keys to* Lolita. Bloomington: Indiana University Press, 1968.
Rafferty, Terrence. Rev. of *Full Metal Jacket*. *Nation* 1/8 Aug. 1987: 98–99.
Ransom, John Crowe. *God without Thunder: An Unorthodox Defense of Orthodoxy*. London: Gerald Howe, 1931.

Reaves, Gerri. "*Full Metal Jacket* and the Beast Within." *Literature/Film Quarterly* 16.4 (1988): 226-36.
Reynolds, Charles. "Interview with Kubrick." *Popular Photography* Dec. 1960: 144+.
Ross, Harris. *Film As Literature, Literature as Film.* Westport, CT: Greenwood Press, 1987.
Sale, Roger. "Love and War." Rev. of *The Short-Timers*, by Gustav Hasford. *New York Times Review of Books* 22 Feb. 1979: 19.
Sarris, Andrew. "Movie Journal." Rev. of Lolita. *Village Voice* 5 July 1962: 11.
Schickel, Richard. "Red Herrings and Refusals." Rev. of *The Shining. Time* 2 June 1980: 69.
Seldes, Gilbert. "The Vandals of Hollywood: Why 'a Good Movie Cannot Be Faithful to the Original Book or Play.'" *Saturday Review of Literature* 17 Oct. 1936: 3-14.
The Shining. Dir. Stanley Kubrick. With Jack Nicholson, Shelley Duvall, Scatman Crothers, and Danny Lloyd. Warner Bros., 1980.
Rev. of *The Shining. Variety* 28 May 1980: 14.
Rev. of *The Shining*, by Stephen King. *Booklist* 1 Mar. 1977: 992.
Rev. of *The Shining*, by Stephen King. *Kirkus Reviews* 1 Dec. 1976: 1277.
Rev. of *The Short-Timers*, by Gustav Hasford. *Kirkus Reviews* 1 Nov. 1978: 1209.
Rev. of *The Short-Timers*, by Gustav Hasford. *Virginia Quarterly Review* 55.3 (1979): 100.
Simon, John. "Horrible Visu." Rev. of *The Shining. National Review* 27 June 1980: 795-97.
———. "Twice-Bitten Bullet." Rev. of *Full Metal Jacket. National Review* 14 Aug 1987: 52-53.
Straczynski, J. Michael. *The Complete Book of Script-Writing.* Cincinnati: Writer's Digest Books, 1982.
Sullivan, Jack. "Two Ways to Write a Gothic." Rev. of *The Shining*, by Stephen King. *New York Times Book Review* 20 Feb. 1977: 8.
Sutton, Walter. *Modern American Criticism.* Englewood Cliffs, NJ: Prentice-Hall, Inc., 1963.
Swain, Dwight V., and Joye R. Swain. *Film Scriptwriting: A Practical Manual.* Stoneham, MA: Butterworth Publishers, 1988.
Thompson, Kristin. *Breaking the Glass Armor: Neoformalist Film Analysis.* Princeton, NJ: Princeton University Press, 1988.
Wald, Jerry. "Screen Adaptation." *Films in Review* 5 (1954): 62-67.
Walker, Alexander. *Sex in the Movies: The Celluloid Sacrifice.* Baltimore: Penguin Books, 1966.
———. *Stanley Kubrick Directs.* New York: Harcourt Brace Jovanovich, 1971.

Westerbeck, Colin L., Jr. "The Waning: Kubrick's Grandiose Hotel." Rev. of *The Shining*. *Commonweal* 1 Aug. 1980: 438–40.
Wichelns, Herbert A. "The Literary Criticism of Oratory." *The Rhetorical Idiom: Essays in Rhetoric, Oratory, Language, and Drama*. Ed. Donald C. Bryant. Ithaca: Cornell University Press, 1958. 5–42.

Index

Allen, Walter 32
Alpert, Hollis 33
Anderson, Carolyn 26, 27
Andrew, Dudley 4–6, 19, 20
Andrews, James 26, 27
Appel, Alfred 33
Aristotle 25
Asheim, Lester 7, 13, 14, 149

Ball, John 71
Barthes, Roland 9
Bauer, Leda 5, 7, 9, 10
Bazin, André 3, 7, 13, 15, 160
Beatty, Jack 108
Beckley, Paul 33
Beja, Morris 5
Benson, Thomas 26, 27
Bergman, Ingmar 18
Bernstein, Jeremy 2
Bhagavad Gita 137
Block, Maxine 5
Bluestone, George 3, 15, 17
Bodeen, DeWitt 21, 22, 161
Booth, Wayne 26
Bordwell, David 27
Brenner, Conrad 32
Bromell, Henry 71, 105
Bryant, Donald 25, 26
Bunzel, Peter 35
Butcher, Maryvonne 6
Bywater, Tim 29

Catch-22 108
Chesterton, G. K. 69
Clarke, Arthur C. 2
Clemons, Walter 108
Conaty, Barbara 87
Conan Doyle, Arthur 5
Corliss, Richard 1, 110, 161
Crichton, Michael 6
Curtis, Francis 108

Deliverance 37
Denby, David 110, 114, 118, 141, 147, 159
Dewey, John 27
Dick, Bernard 18, 161
Dispatches 109
Duffy, Martha 2
Durgnat, Raymond 41
Dwan, Allan 20

Edison, Thomas 5
Eidsvik, Charles 17, 18
Eliot, T. S. 27, 28, 47
Enser's Filmed Books and Plays 5

Fadiman, William 6, 8, 11, 12
Field, Alice Evans 10, 11, 160
Fitzgerald, F. Scott 18
Freud, Sigmund 52
Full Metal Jacket 1–3, 29, 107, 109–147, 151–160

Index

Geduld, Harry 5
Godfrey, Lionel 12, 153
Goldman, William 22

Hartung, Phillip 33, 39
Hasford, Gustav 107–109, 116, 118, 124, 140, 150
Heller, Joseph 108
"Hello, Vietnam" 110, 111
Hemingway, Ernest 12, 109
Herr, Michael 109
Horne, William 3, 5, 7
Hughes, Riley 31
humanism 26, 29

Iser, Wolfgang 6

Jameson, Richard 72, 79, 83, 95
Janeway, Elizabeth 33
Jung, Carl 109, 134

Kael, Pauline 95, 102, 109, 110
Kagan, Norman 1, 2
Kauffmann, Stanley 72
Kazan, Elia 18
King, Stephen 69–73, 82, 86, 87, 94, 102, 105, 149, 150
Kinney, Judy Lee 3
Kirkus Reviews 71, 108
Kubrick, Stanley 1–3, 9, 23–25, 32–37, 39, 40, 43, 44, 47, 49, 52–55, 60, 62, 63, 66, 68, 70–73, 75, 78, 82, 86, 87, 90, 91, 93–95, 100–102, 105, 108–112, 119–128, 130, 135, 137–143, 145–147, 149–161

Lacayo, Richard 108, 110, 147
Larsson, Donald 18, 19
Lingeman, Richard 71, 87
Lolita (film) 1, 2, 3, 29, 34–68, 72, 105, 111, 150–154, 156–160

Lolita (novel) 24, 31–68, 70, 150, 152–154, 156–159
Lyon, Sue 40

Macbeth 138
McCaffrey, Donald 15, 16, 161
MacDonald, Dwight 34, 52
McFarlane, Brian 6, 7
Madsen, Roy Paul 16, 17
Marion, Frances 10, 11
Max, D. T. 12, 13
Mitry, Jean 16
Molnar, Thomas 32, 33

Nabokov, Vladimir 31–35, 39, 41, 47, 52–55, 59, 60, 63, 68, 70, 72, 150, 157, 159, 161
Nelson, Thomas 1
neoformalism 26, 28
New Criticism 26–28
Nicholson, Jack 72, 80, 99
Niebuhr, Reinhold 36

objective correlative 23, 47, 62, 140, 153
O'Brien, Tom 110, 147
One Flew Over the Cuckoo's Nest 72
Oppenheimer, J. Robert 137
Orwell, George 23, 69
Owen, Wilfred 145

Phillips, Gene 2
Pinter, Harold 18
Poe, Edgar Allan 44, 74
Pollock, Tom 13, 33
Pope, Alexander 105
Proffer, Carl 159
Psycho 127

Rafferty, Terrence 111, 112, 141
Ransom, John Crowe 27, 28
Reaves, Gerri 110

rhetoric 1, 25–29, 79, 83, 98, 102, 104, 105, 111, 116, 118, 145, 147, 156, 160, 161
Ross, Harris 5

Sale, Roger 108
Sarris, Andrew 52
Schickel, Richard 2
Seldes, Gilbert 6–8, 10
Sellers, Peter 50, 56, 57
"The Sentinel" 2
The Shining (film) 1, 2, 29, 71–105, 108, 126, 128, 149–160
The Shining (novel) 69–96, 98–105, 111, 149, 150, 152–158
Shklovsky, Viktor 28, 67
The Short-Timers 107–147, 150, 152, 153, 155–159
Simon, John 71, 79, 110, 147
Smith, Scott 6, 12
Sobchack, Thomas 29
Spielberg, Steven 6

Swain, Dwight 8, 22
Swain, Judy 8, 22

Taradash, David 21
Tevis, Walter 12
Thompson, Kristin 29, 55, 67
2001: A Space Odyssey 2, 70

"Ulalume" 44

Variety 33, 34, 71, 72
The Virginia Quarterly Review 108

Wald, Jerry 20, 21
Walker, Alexander 2, 32
Westerbeck, Colin 70
Wichelns, Herbert 34
Winters, Shelley 39, 43, 48, 50
Wright, Johnny 110

www.ingramcontent.com/pod-product-compliance
Ingram Content Group UK Ltd.
Pitfield, Milton Keynes, MK11 3LW, UK
UKHW042016140426
5217IPUK00015B/1198